Richard Wilbur

in conversation with

Peter Dale

Richard Wilbur

in conversation with

Peter Dale

Between The Lines

First published in 2000 by

Between The Lines

9 Woodstock Road
London N4 3ET
UK

Tel: +44 (0)20 7272 8719
Fax: +44 (0)20 8374 5736

E-mail: betweenthelines@lineone.net
Website: http://www.interviews-with-poets.com

© Questions: Peter Dale
© Answers: Richard Wilbur
© 'Mayflies': Richard Wilbur
© Photograph of Richard Wilbur: Stathis Orphanos
© Photograph of the baroque wall fountain, Villa Sciarra, Rome: Philip Hoy

The right of Peter Dale to be identified as the author of this work
has been asserted by him in accordance with
the Copyright, Designs and Patents Act of 1988

All rights reserved

A CIP catalogue record for this book
is available from the British Library

ISBN 0 9532841 5 8

Jacket design and artwork: Philip Hoy

Printed and bound by

RPM Reprographics Ltd
2-3 Spur Road
Quarry Lane
Chichester
West Sussex
PO19 2PR

Between The Lines

EDITORIAL BOARD

PETER DALE — IAN HAMILTON — PHILIP HOY — J.D. MCCLATCHY

BTL publishes unusually wide-ranging and unusually deep-going interviews with some of today's most accomplished poets.

Some would deny that any useful purpose is served by putting to a writer questions which are not answered by that writer's books. For them, what Yeats called 'the bundle of accident and incoherence that sits down to breakfast' is best left alone, not asked to interrupt its cornflakes, or to set aside its morning paper, while someone with a tape recorder inquires about its life, habits and attitudes.

If we do not share this view, it is not because we endorse Sainte-Beuve's dictum, *tel arbre, tel fruit* — *as the tree, so the fruit* — but because we understand what Geoffrey Braithwaite was getting at when the author of *Flaubert's Parrot* had him say:

> 'But if you love a writer, if you depend upon the drip-feed of his intelligence, if you want to pursue him and find him — despite edicts to the contrary — then it's impossible to know too much.'

The first six volumes, featuring W.D. Snodgrass, Michael Hamburger, Anthony Thwaite, Anthony Hecht, Donald Hall, and Thom Gunn, respectively, are already available; others now being prepared will feature Seamus Heaney, Paul Muldoon, Donald Justice and Hans Magnus Enzensberger. (Further details are given overleaf.)

As well as the interview, each volume will contain a sketch of the poet's life and career, a comprehensive bibliography, archival information, and a representative selection of quotations from the poet's critics and reviewers. It is hoped that the results will be of interest to the lay reader and specialist alike.

– Other volumes from BTL –

W.D. Snodgrass
in conversation with Philip Hoy
ISBN 0-9532841-0-7

Michael Hamburger
in conversation with Peter Dale
ISBN 0-9532841-1-5

Anthony Thwaite
in conversation with Peter Dale and Ian Hamilton
ISBN 0-9532841-2-3

Anthony Hecht
in conversation with Philip Hoy
ISBN 0-9532841-3-1

Donald Hall
in conversation with Ian Hamilton
ISBN 0-9532841-4-X

Thom Gunn
in conversation with James Campbell
ISBN 1 903291 00 3

– Forthcoming –

Seamus Heaney
in conversation with Karl Miller
ISBN 0-9532841-7-4

Paul Muldoon
in conversation with Lavinia Greenlaw
ISBN 0-9532841-8-2

Donald Justice
in conversation with Philip Hoy
ISBN 0-9532841-9-0

Hans Magnus Enzensberger
in conversation with Michael Hulse and John Kinsella
ISBN 0-9532841-6-6

Contents

Acknowledgements	9
A Portrait of Richard Wilbur	10
A Note on Richard Wilbur	11
A Note on Peter Dale	15
The Conversation	17
'Mayflies' by Richard Wilbur	65
Bibliography	67
The Critics	89

Acknowledgements

The editors would like to thank Richard Wilbur for permission to reprint the poem which appears on page 65, Stathis Orphanos for permission to use the photograph which appears on page 10, and Meredith Arthur of Harcourt, New York, for speedy dispatch of an advance reading copy of *Mayflies*.

They would also like to thank John Lancaster and Jack W.C. Hagstrom, who generously made available the bibliographical information – extracted from their full descriptive bibliography, in preparation – which appears on pages 67-88.

Finally, they would like to thank John Lancaster for the care with which he proof-read the bibliography after it had been modified so as to conform to English rather than American conventions. (If any typographical errors are found, the reader can be sure that they were introduced by us subsequently.)

Richard Wilbur

Photograph courtesy of
Stathis Orphanos

©

A Note on Richard Wilbur

Richard Wilbur was born in New York City in 1921, the first son of Lawrence Lazear and Helen Ruth Wilbur (née Purdy). When he was two years old, the family moved to North Caldwell, a small town in New Jersey, where he and his younger brother Lawrence grew up in rural surroundings.

Wilbur was attracted to painting in his youth, but eventually chose to pursue writing instead, something he attributes to the influence of two people – his mother's father, and her grandfather, both of whom worked in the newspaper business. As a schoolboy, he wrote editorials, stories and poems for Montclair High School's newspaper and magazine, and as an undergraduate, he contributed stories and poems to Amherst College's student magazine, *Touchstone,* as well as editing the campus newspaper, *The Amherst Student.*

In 1942, Wilbur graduated from Amherst, married Mary Charlotte Hayes Ward, and signed up for the Enlisted Reserve Corps. Sent to Europe the following year, he joined the 36th (Texas) Infantry Division, and saw action, first at Monte Cassino, later at Anzio, and later still along the Siegfried Line. It was during this period that he began, as he described it later, 'to versify in earnest'.

After the war, Wilbur went to Harvard to study for an MA. He graduated in 1947, and that year published his first collection, *The Beautiful Changes and Other Poems.* The book was enthusiastically reviewed by Louise Bogan, Babette Deutsch, Richard Eberhart, Robert Fitzgerald, M.L. Rosenthal, and other critics of note, and caused Wilbur to be spoken of in the same breath as Robert Lowell, whose *Lord Weary's Castle* had been published to great acclaim the year before, and whose penchant for formality bore a superficial resemblance to Wilbur's own.

Wilbur spent the next three years as a member of the Society of Fellows at Harvard. Then, in 1950, the year in which he was appointed Assistant Professor at the university, he published his second collection, *Ceremony and Other Poems.* This book was also well received, with David Daiches, John Frederick Nims, Peter Viereck and others joining in the chorus of praise. One influential critic did sound a discordant note, however, and that was Randall Jarrell. While allowing that Wilbur was the best of the younger poets then writing, and commending him for his lyric and descriptive powers, Jarrell nevertheless proposed that he was 'not a very satisfactory poet', arguing that '[m]ost of his poetry consents too easily to its own unnecessary limitations.'

From 1955 until 1957, Wilbur was Professor at Wellesley College in Massachusetts. In his second year there, his third collection, *Things of This World*, appeared. Donald Hall declared that the book contained 'the best poems Wilbur has yet written', and he wasn't alone in his judgement: John Ciardi, Paul Engle and Anthony Hecht all spoke highly of it. *Things of This World* won that year's National Book Award, as well as the Pulitzer Prize.

Shortly before arriving at Wellesley, Wilbur had been approached by Leonard Bernstein and Lillian Hellman, and asked to produce lyrics for the comic operetta they were working on, *Candide*. The collaboration, though fruitful, was not always easy. Bernstein evidently thought well of his own abilities as a writer, with the result that a sorely-tried Wilbur had once to tell Hellman, 'If you catch [Lenny] re-writing my lyrics, clip his piano wires.'

After leaving Wellesley, Wilbur went to Wesleyan University in Connecticut, where, in addition to teaching and writing, he was responsible for initiating and then advising on the University Press's poetry programme, something whose success led other university presses to set up poetry lists of their own.

Wilbur remained at Wesleyan for almost twenty years, and during that time published three more collections of verse – *Advice to a Prophet and Other Poems* (1961), *Walking to Sleep* (1969) and *The Mind-Reader* (1976) – as well as a collection of critical essays, *Responses* (1976). Many more honours also came his way, amongst them: the Edna St Vincent Millay Award (1957), a Ford Fellowship (1960), the Melville Cane Award (1962), two Bollingen Prizes (1963 and 1971), the Sarah Josepha Hale Award (1968), the Brandeis University Creative Arts Award (1970), the Henri Desfeuilles Prize (1971), and the Shelley Memorial Award (1973).

Of the two Bollingen Prizes listed above, the first was awarded for work in a field for which Wilbur was to become especially noted – translation. The verse translation of Molière's *Tartuffe* which secured him the prize had been preceded by a verse translation of the same writer's *The Misanthrope* – it was the critical success of this that had brought Wilbur to the attention of Bernstein and Hellman – and by translations of poems by Valéry, de Thaun, Jammes, Baudelaire, Nerval, Quasimodo and Guillén. Later still, Wilbur would turn his hand to translating Molière's *The School for Wives, The Learned Ladies, The School for Husbands, Sganarelle, or The Imaginary Cuckold, Amphitryon, Don Juan* and *The Bungler*, Racine's *Andromaque* and *Phèdre*, and poems by the still more diverse grouping of Villon, d'Orléans, Vosnesensky, Akhmatova, Borges, Morshen, Brodsky, Voltaire, du Bellay, La Fontaine, Apollinaire, de Moraes, Baudelaire, Petrov, Dante, Cassian and Mallarmé.

Between 1977 and 1986, Wilbur was back in Massachusetts, as Writer in Residence at Smith College, where his wife had once been a student. Though he published no new collections during this period, three of his Molière translations did appear, along with a quantity of critical and other work, including his edition of Witter Bynner's *Selected Poems*. The list of honours also lengthened, with the addition of the Harriet Monroe Award (1978), the PEN Translation Award (1983), the Drama Desk Award for Translation (1983), the St Botolph's Club Foundation Award (1983), and a Camargo Foundation Fellowship (1985).

In 1987, Wilbur succeeded Robert Penn Warren and became Poet Laureate of the United States. In its earlier incarnations – as Chair in Poetry and then Consultancy in Poetry to the Library of Congress – this post had been held by a string of distinguished figures – amongst them Robert Frost, Randall Jarrell, Elizabeth Bishop and Anthony Hecht – so when William Logan, one of America's more astringent critics, declared that 'the honour [done to Wilbur] was not misplaced', readers knowing something about the British Laureateship and nothing about the American should not suppose that he was being ironic.

By this time, though, Wilbur will have grown accustomed to seeing himself written off by his more hostile critics, described as an *empty formalist, eloquent anachronism,* or some such. What Robert von Hallberg said in an essay written for *The Cambridge History of American Literature* is not untypical: 'A number of features of 1950s verse are epitomized in [Wilbur's] style. His poems are deliberately ornate, obviously rich in consonance and assonance, superficially indebted to Hopkins. His language is insistently figurative. Everything is seen in terms of something else – "this mad *instead*", he calls it in a self-critical moment. To emblems, similes, and pretty phrases, he is devoted – to just those types of figurative language that make no claim to spontaneity or sudden revelation. His poems constantly offer the charm of wit, but rarely the force of conviction.'

In 1988, however, twelve years after *The Mind-Reader*, Wilbur's *New and Collected Poems* appeared, and a number of its reviewers called for a reappraisal, urging that, as one of them put it, 'there are poems throughout ... that will take any preconception by surprise, poems ... that we've had in mind and by heart for years, the first sign that a book is likely to remain a classic.' The same critic, nodding in the direction of Wilbur's detractors, also pointed out that 'if there is sometimes too much varnish, the draftsmanship is always impeccable, the composition noble, the colouring warm and affecting.'

With the publication of *New and Collected Poems*, Wilbur's list of honours lengthened once again, this time with the addition of a Bunn Award (1988), the Washington College Literature Award (1988), the St Louis Literature Award (1988), the Taylor Poetry Award (1988), the *Los Angeles Times* Book Prize (1988), and a second Pulitzer Prize (1989). The book also secured a nomination for the National Book Critics Circle Award (1988).

Since 1988, Wilbur has published a second volume of essays, *The Catbird's Song* (1997). He has also received the Gold Medal Award for Poetry from the American Academy and Institute of Arts and Letters (1991), the Edward MacDowell Medal (1992), the National Arts Club Medal of Honour for Literature (1994), the PEN/Manheim Medal for Translation (1995), the Milton Center Prize (1995), and the American Academy Achievement Award (1995).

Wilbur's eighth volume of poems, *Mayflies,* was published by Harcourt in April 2000, a few weeks after the poet celebrated his seventy-ninth birthday.

A Note on Peter Dale

Peter Dale was born in Surrey in 1938, and educated at Strode's School, Egham, and St Peter's College, Oxford, where he read English. He ran a large English Department in one of the first comprehensive schools from 1972 until 1993, and with William Cookson edited *Agenda* over the same period, amongst other things preparing issues on rhythm, rhyme, Stanley Burnshaw, the Sixties, the Seventies, and the state of poetry.

Dale's verse publications include: *The Storms* (Macmillan, London, 1968); *Mortal Fire* (Macmillan, London, 1970); *Mortal Fire: Selected Poems* (Ohio University Press, USA, 1976); *One Another* (Carcanet New Press, Manchester/Agenda Editions, London, 1978); *Too Much of Water* (Agenda Editions, London, 1983); *Earth Light* (Hippopotamus Press, Frome, 1991). His most recent book of verse is *Edge to Edge: Selected Poems* (Anvil, London, 1996).

He has also published several books of formal verse translation: *Villon* (Macmillan, London/St Martins Press, New York, 1973); *Selected Poems of François Villon* (Penguin, London, 1978/Viking, New York, 1988); *Poems of Jules Laforgue* (Anvil, London, 1986). His single-volume, terza-rima version of *The Divine Comedy* appeared from Anvil in 1996, and was reprinted with some revisions in 1998.

Other books include *An Introduction to Rhyme* (Bellew/Agenda Editions, London, 1998), *Michael Hamburger in Conversation with Peter Dale* (BTL, London, 1998), and *Anthony Thwaite in Conversation with Peter Dale and Ian Hamilton* (BTL, London, 1999).

Scheduled for 2000 are revised and enlarged editions of *Poems of Jules Laforgue* (Anvil, London) and *The Poems of François Villon* (Anvil, London).

Dale is currently a member of the committee of The Translators' Association.

The Conversation

Early in 1999, Richard Wilbur was sent a list of almost ninety questions. He was told that there was no hurry, and that he should take up only those questions that interested him. His answers were received in instalments, the first arriving in July, and others following in the autumn and winter. A small number of supplementary questions were sent in January 2000, shortly after BTL received an advance reading copy of Wilbur's latest collection, *Mayflies*. What the poet, in a letter accompanying his last set of answers, called his and his interviewer's 'typewriter badminton' came to an end in March, 2000.

You have given many interviews – at least a sizable book full, edited by William Butts in 1990 – so that it will be difficult to avoid overlaps here. Let's get the inevitable preliminaries over and try to find some newer angles as we go. Can you tell us something about your childhood and upbringing – in a fairly rural setting, I believe?

Though born in New York City, I spent my childhood in a New Jersey country town called North Caldwell which was twenty miles from New York and has now been wiped out by spreading suburbs. In 1922 or so, my artist father was introduced on the golf course to Joshua Dickinson Armitage, a British textile manufacturer who had greatly prospered in America. Mr Armitage took a liking to him, and offered him at low rental a pre-Revolutionary stone house on the grounds of a 450-acre gentleman's farm which he had constructed in rural New Jersey. That's how we got there. Mr Armitage, as he often told us, had been patronized in England for being 'in trade', and his country estate – with its beautiful tile-roofed barns, sheds, and other buildings, its fields and gardens, its orchards, its bull-pens, pigsties and stone-walled lanes – was in part a compensation for that. What made the farm gentlemanly were the big house on the hill, the swimming pool, the tennis court and the two bowling greens. The farm and its vicinity were peopled, on the whole, with Mr Armitage's relatives, employees, and business associates, and the atmosphere was British-colonial.

I grew up among kind and lively people, many of whom I called Aunt or Uncle. The farm hands were good to me and my younger brother, and let us interfere in all of their operations – haying, silage-making, apple-picking, pig-slaughtering, and the rest. I climbed trees, fell out of them, rambled in the woods. At night, there was a quietness now rare in American experience: there was the occasional moo or hoof-knock from the barn; the passing of a car on our dirt road was an event; sometimes the clank of trolley-car brakes came on the wind from Caldwell, two and a half miles away. My childhood left me with a preference for living in the sticks, for long walks, for physical work and the raising of great crops of herbs and vegetables. It made me a fair amateur naturalist and gave me an ability – essential in a poet, I should think – to make something of solitude.

Auden says of Rimbaud 'the cold had made a poet'. But it wasn't like that with you, I think. People are usually set going by poems they read or hear – or by some teacher or other introducer. Were there any family leanings in literary directions or was there opposition to your idea of being a poet?

A maternal great-grandfather, Horace Purdy, was an itinerant newspaper editor who dragged his fonts of type all over the Middle West, not leaving any town or city until its only (or prevailing) journal was Democratic. He founded forty papers in that way, or so his obituary claimed. His son, C. M. Purdy – a wonderful, slight, peppery man – was city editor of the *Baltimore Sun* and worked on that paper into his eighties. You can see that, from my mother's side, our house inherited a respect for writing. My father, during my young years, was a successful commercial artist who commuted to a studio on 23rd Street in New York, and there did magazine covers, illustrations, and advertisements, employing as models such people as Brian Donleavy, Charles Atlas, and a succession of Miss Rheingolds. When he got tired of commerce and the colour limitations of lithography, he became a truly fine portrait painter in the tradition of his teacher Robert Henri. There was nothing very arty or literary about my family, but my parents were encouraging about anything one happened to draw, or write, or play.

Which poets provided you with your earliest enthusiasms?

The Poetry Society of America has just asked me the same question, and, after mentioning Stevenson and Lewis Carroll, I said this: 'There was in my parents' house an anthology called *Poems of American Patriotism*, and I think that such splendid public poems as Whittier's 'Barbara Frietchie' so conditioned me that I would never be able to associate poetry with, for instance, breathy personal confidences in free verse.' As an adolescent, though I didn't yet suppose myself to be chiefly a poet, I was devoted to Joyce, Crane, Frost and Eliot – not understanding the last very well, but relishing his texture of tones and voices. Reading Crane made me feel drunk. I bought, in New York City's second hand bookstores, back numbers of *Transition*, in which I responded to the explosive, liberating spirit (though not always to the execution) of Dada and Surrealist poetry. One hopeful thing about me in those days was that, while my political sympathies were with the left, and I admired the artwork in the *New Masses*, I never supposed that right-minded indignation could do the work of imagination and technical performance. Lines like 'Conscript negroes march at dawn to the uranium mines' never seemed to me excusable. Later, that attitude kept me – though I actively resisted my country's Vietnam adventure – from writing rally-pleasing anti-war poems.

Your remark about the New Masses *magazine makes me wonder whether you knew one of its editors, Stanley Burnshaw? He edited* The Poem Itself, *on translation, which you're probably familiar with, and also did a book,* Robert Frost Himself, *as a counter to Lawrance Thompson's vindictive biography.*

Oh, I greatly admire Burnshaw's *The Poem Itself*, and corresponded with him when he was writing the Frost book. And I recall meeting him in '59, at Robert Frost's eighty-fifth birthday party, when Lionel Trilling's speech created such a fuss and furore ...

Because he said that Frost's poems dealt with 'the terrible actualities of life,' that, so far from being the comforting figure many people thought, he was actually 'a terrifying poet'.

I recall saying to the agitated Robert, 'It was kindly meant.'

What about your university years? You did your first degree at Amherst. How was that?

Amherst College's fine English department taught me that, if I read carefully and hard, I could actually interact on my own with Andrew Marvell or John Bunyan. That was exciting, and made me think of scholar-critic as a possible good thing to become. At the same time I was editing the undergraduate newspaper, drawing cartoons, and writing both verse and fiction, so that I was by no means focused on any one future profession. People have often wondered why Amherst, which in my day had no 'creative writing' classes to speak of, has produced so many poets – James Merrill, David Ferry, and Robert Bagg among them. I suspect it has had something to do with the local shade of Emily Dickinson, and the long association of Robert Frost with the college – but still more to do with the fact that one's best teachers found time to read and commend good undergraduate poetry, and that one's classmates, though not a bunch of aesthetes, had a civilized esteem for the art.

Friendships one makes at this stage can be pretty central, even crucial, to a writer's career and development. Did you make many literary friends?

At Amherst, I covered up a certain social awkwardness by carousing and being outrageous. A few of my friends were literary, and would go on to be writers or teachers, but I belonged to a fraternity which specialized in football, and I had friends of all sorts. Harvard – whose graduate school of English I went to after World War II, as a veteran financed by the 'G. I. Bill' – was a different matter. There my wife and I were part of a wave of young people who had given years to beating the Axis, and who were starved for arts and letters and for talk about those things. Harvard teachers were great scholars and peerless advisors, but their classes, which consisted largely of lectures read from old notebooks or 5-by-7 cards, were often dull – or less inspiring, at any rate, than the bingeing literary enthusiasm of my fellow-veterans, many of whom became lifelong friends.

And what about enemies and animosities? They're easily made in such hotbeds of learning. How well did you cope with all that?

At the risk of seeming characterless and ingratiating, I confess that I had no enemies at Amherst, and have never much dealt in personal animosities. During the war, I recall being annoyed by the prissy clerkishness of a fellow-sergeant who was promoted ahead of me; yet I couldn't quite manage to ignore his good qualities. A composer with whom I collaborated in the '50s was sometimes self-interested and devious, but he was undeniably brilliant and full of life. A real-estate rascal of the 1970s, with whom I unwisely had a 'gentleman's agreement', could perhaps have become the object of a full-blown hatred had he not, in the manner of such opportunists, moved on to another town. I have it in me to hate, and if I have been lucky enough not to do too much of that, it is probably because I have not too often been wronged, balked, or humiliated. In my most memorable experience of hatred, which occurred during a Swan cruise of the Mediterranean, I was the object. A Scots doctor, who was a fellow-passenger, conceived an intense unspoken dislike for me – on the basis of what, I do not know. It is true that I sometimes wore red trousers; it is true that, thinking myself alone, I ran a couple of laps around the amphitheatre at Cos, and was crowned with a wreath of something by some ladies; but really I have no idea how I had led or enabled him to detest me. He could not keep his baleful eyes off me. When he was meant to be admiring mosaics in a Patmos chapel, he was glaring sidewise at me; when he should have been studying the defensive system of Mycenae, he was staring at me and, I think, inwardly muttering something on the order of Browning's 'Soliloquy of the Spanish Cloister'. A gloating antipathy of that sort is a sad thing; it shrinks consciousness, shrinks the heart and is a damned waste of time.

Of course there are qualities, as opposed to whole persons, which I wholeheartedly dislike: mendacity, smugness, cruelty, stinginess, chic vulgarity. I find sanctimony and cocksure atheism equally disagreeable. Politically, my enemies are big-money Republicans, legislators who are essentially lobbyists, land speculators, ruthless entrepreneurs generally.

You did military service from 1943-45, only a year after getting married, some of it, I believe, in France and Germany. Was this a difficult time?

It was difficult to say goodbye to a wife and new-born daughter but I had come to have no doubt that our war was just and necessary. Further difficulty attended my early stateside months in the Army when, after basic infantry training and a course in cryptography, I was sent to a secret cryptanalytic camp in the woods of Virginia, and then bounced out of there (after a bit of commando training) because the FBI and the CIC had concluded that I was a radical. Actually, my political ideas were ordinary leftish ones, Rooseveltian and entirely patriotic; but I was told after the war, by a prep-school headmaster who had helped to devise the Army's security policy, that what the armed forces ideally wanted, for the purposes of secret work, was a bright person who somehow had no political notions whatever. I was sent off, with 'suspected of disloyalty' stamped on my service record, to a camp in Chenango, Pennsylvania, a vast dumping ground for undesirables, and thence was sent overseas, with an ad hoc company of amiable undesirables, as a general replacement. Arriving (by way of Bizerte) at a replacement depot in a racetrack near Naples, I expected to be sent into a line company as a rifleman, yet untrained in the Garand. (Our boot camp in the States had done its teaching with old Enfields.) Providentially, however, a cryptographer in the 36th (Texas) Division had just gone mad, and I found myself being interviewed in the tent of Captain Wingo of the 36th Division Signal Company, who had my record before him on the desk.

'Private Wilbur reporting for duty, sir.'

'Private Wilbur, it says on this report that you want to overthrow the government. Is that so?'

'No, sir, I don't want to overthrow the government.'

'All right, then. We need a cryptographer. But if I catch you overthrowing the government, out you go.'

That exchange may seem to have been polished into good comic dialogue, and it's my impression that many reminiscences of war take fear and horror for granted, and shape their material into funny stories. It was good to spend the war with country Texans, who are good soldiers and original talkers. After I joined the Division, we went first to Monte Cassino, where we took bad losses in the line companies; then pulled back and went up the coast to Anzio, tipping the balance there. We had the pleasure of taking Rome. Next, we returned to the south and made ready for an amphibious invasion of France, going ashore without difficulty at

Frejus and San Raphael. The Germans having withdrawn, that landing was so easy that I spent the afternoon of it sitting in the library of a summer mansion and reading a mediaeval text called *Helmbrecht le Fermier*. Finally, after we had pushed far to the north, we had a cold winter along the Siegfried Line.

Anthony Hecht also served in the army, and saw action in Europe, at this time. He evidently witnessed some terrible things, and was deeply affected. How did you cope?

I had been prepared to enjoy, in war, its knockabout, adventurous character, because as a young man I had travelled all over the States in freight trains, sleeping on roadsides, in jails, and in hobo jungles. Moments of solidarity and unit pride somewhat countered our frights and losses and the general dreadfulness. But what most helped me get through two years in a division which had little rest, was having the hang of certain necessary things. I think that's how it is with everyone who is able to preserve his morale. I'd come into the Army with some knowledge of cryptography and radio physics. I was slow but competent as a Morse code operator. I could use a teletype, which (because I had a few words of French) came in handy when we were for a time under the French First Army; I could be taught to lay a wire down to the line companies, and was. But my small special ability lay in solving enciphered messages, sent to us in five-letter code groups and messed up by poor transmission or reception; with my knowledge of Morse, I was often able to guess what letters had been garbled, and so go on deciphering to the end. A puzzle-solving temperament can serve to focus and insulate one, in war or out.

You have said in a broadcast for Voice of America, later published in Shenandoah (xvii.1, 1965), under the title 'On My Own Work', 'My first poems were written in answer to the inner and outer disorders of the Second World War, and they helped me, as poems should, to take a hold of raw events and convert them, provisionally, into experience.' This seems to suggest a more central therapeutic role for poetry than some of the current 'ludic' or language-based poets would accept or admit.

Poetry being the organizing art which one can practise in a foxhole, I and countless other soldiers have made use of it. A lot of apprentice efforts, as you suppose, were excluded from my first book, and I've tended not to borrow from them, though I recall what gave them rise.
    Language poetry, as I understand it, is based on mistrust of such concepts as author, text, and intention; if so, it's an exaggeration of com-

plexities of which poets have always been aware, and doesn't justify giving up on the ancient functions of the art and simply diddling. I don't suppose that there's been a more 'ludic' or playful poet than Stevens, who was for a time dismissed as a lightweight 'dandy' and who did not appear at all in Bliss Carman's hospitable *Oxford Book of American Verse* back in 1927. But it was Stevens who wrote, 'How gladly with proper words the soldier dies', and who thought of poetry, in a larger sense to which specific poems are tributary, as a culture's articulate sense of itself. Good poems, I think, release us from inarticulateness, which is a great misery, challenge us to tell the whole truth of ourselves and others, and are taken up into that overarching poetry of which Stevens speaks.

Did your wartime experience of Europe incline you to your later interest in translating, largely from French?

Though my spoken French was (as it still is) pretty awkward, I often served as unofficial company interpreter during our campaign in France; I picked up books and papers as we went, read Loti and Aragon, tried to read Mallarmé. I remember that I felt a naive wonder at being in a country where the beautiful words I had been taught in school were lettered over storefronts, and otherwise put to common use. But the inclination to translate from French really dates from my early postwar years at Harvard, when two friends – André du Bouchet and Pierre Schneider – led me to read certain French authors (Villiers, Roussel, Nerval) and challenged me to render this or that into English. I recall the pleasure of sitting in our Cambridge living-room with André (now an august figure in French poetry) and translating each other's youthful poems. He could manage sometimes to make me sound like Baudelaire.

How difficult was it to settle down back in America after the war? Did you, did acquaintances, have problems like some of the Vietnam veterans in making the readjustment to civilian life again?

It wasn't difficult at all. It's true that I left the army with some $400 in my pocket, and a wife and child to support, and no firm notion of how I was going to make a living. But one came back to an approving and applauding nation which wanted to give the veteran every possible break – one such break being, in my case, free graduate training in a profession which I decided to enter. The poor veterans of Vietnam, by contrast, had fought in a fruitless war which was widely denounced, and from which middle-class college students had self-righteously excused themselves. The Vietnam boys came back, feeling scorned, to a country which wanted to forget about them. Perhaps they received certain tangible benefits from the nation, but what they didn't get was goodwill or gratitude.

How did you make your entry into university teaching? Many British poets only made it by going abroad – which imposed an exile of sorts (though as Julio Cortazar has said, 'The only true exile is the writer who lives in his own country').

It was my good luck, after a year of graduate courses, to be taken into Harvard's Society of Fellows, which had been conceived by its President Lowell as an alternative to the doctoral programme. That meant three years of independent work, lively luncheons with twenty-odd other young scholars from various fields, and weekly dinners during which one talked with splendid, formidable Senior Fellows like Alfred North Whitehead and Samuel Eliot Morison. During those three years I pursued and then abandoned a study of dandyism in literature, did a lot of work on Poe, and wrote a second book of poems. Like many Junior Fellows before me, I went on into the Harvard faculty. My later teaching – at Wellesley, Wesleyan, and Smith – was always within New England, where I wanted to be, and so I never felt an exile.

Actually, one thing about the United States is that it has no Paris – no centre where one must be, where all the best action is; and though some regions and regional cultures are more agreeable than others, there is so wide a scattering of brains and talent that an American poet-teacher might feel at home more or less anywhere in the country. One learns this by flying around and giving readings: even when one is visiting some quite unheard-of college, the chances are that bright faces will be there to meet the plane.

Poets, I think, have a kind of love-hate relationship with the academic way of life, and in recent years there's perhaps been more hate than love, given all the emphasis on 'theory'. In a previous interview in this series, Anthony Hecht said how difficult he'd found it in the years before he retired, the many pressure groups who'd established toeholds inside English departments having gone on to trample literature underfoot. Did you find the university environment and teaching community conducive to poetry or something to be surmounted?

When I went to Harvard's graduate school in 1946, I was spoiling to become a scholar, especially of 17th century English and European arts and letters. I never did become as much of a scholar and critic as I then hoped to be – poetry and theatre derailed that – and my chief academic accomplishment is that my several essays on Poe are acknowledged to have opened up a fresh understanding of him. However, I was always enough of a scholar to teach chiefly subject-matter courses, rather than courses in writing: at Harvard and thereafter I taught great-books courses (which had the blessed effect of making this slow reader read great books), courses in Milton or Shakespeare, seminars in Poe or Yeats, that sort of thing. Teaching is hard work, and if one largely teaches subjects rather than writing it requires much reading; but one gets educated and refreshed that way. Classes in verse-writing have always given me some pleasure in the students and their work, but I am glad not to have toiled in the ghetto (so I would have found it) of a creative writing programme. Though I know that many excellent poets have taught in such programmes, I can't help feeling that the courses often adjust their demands to the untalented, are too confined to the contemporary, and don't much instruct the instructor.

I haven't talked with Tony Hecht about his latter years of teaching, though I knew that he had encountered vexations. Every now and then, academic criticism gets to thinking that it is brainier than mere poetry or fiction. That appeared to be the case, for a time, with the New Criticism; how primitive we writers seemed beside the sophistications of a Blackmur! The brilliance of the New Critics, however, was directed toward the elucidation of poems and stories, and their effect was finally enhancing. It would be harder for a poet to be collegial with the 'theory'-critics I hear about nowadays, who think that poets don't know what they're doing, who disallow the text in favour of subtext or agenda, and who themselves have agendas – Marxist, feminist, or other.

While on the subject of your teaching career, but probably out of sequence, may I ask about your time at Wesleyan University – 1957-77 – your main years of teaching? There was a strong, keen interest in supporting new poetry with prizes, publishing and programmes of reading and visits, and I wondered how this came about, and what your role in it was.

I have a framed something-or-other on the wall, given me by the Wesleyan University Press in 1984; it states that the Press's poetry programme was initiated, back in '59, at my suggestion. I guess it was. I can remember saying to the first editors of the new Press that, though they couldn't initially vie with Harvard or Yale for the best scholarly manuscripts, they could achieve distinction at once by publishing some of the outstanding verse which might be theirs for the asking. The Press decided to do that. What they needed was conversancy and taste, and to that end they recruited such advisors and readers as Norman Pearson, Howard Nemerov, John Hollander, Denise Levertov, John Brinnin, Archie Ammons, Louis Simpson, Bill Meredith, Don Hall ... the list of those who served is splendid and very long. Wesleyan's poetry series was a success, even in the financial sense, and it led to readings and festivals at Wesleyan and to the establishment of comparable programmes at other academic presses. It was onerous to read several hundred poetry manuscripts a year, as we all did. But it was exciting to be doing something worthy, effectual, and mysteriously well-timed.

You received recognition as a poet fairly early on, with very positive reviews, and then honours and awards of one kind and another. You must have enjoyed this at the time, but would you agree that early adulation can create problems for a writer? Another of the poets in this series, W.D. Snodgrass, found that the success of his first book set up high and rather fixed expectations, expectations it was very difficult to cope with. You touch lightly on this issue in 'Flippancies, 1: The Star System', but I wonder if I can ask you to comment on it here?

Adulation would be a bad thing for a young writer. It could be paralyzing, it could make him want to do the same lovable thing over and over. What I received, on the whole, was encouragement rather than adulation. One can feel encouraged and at the same time feel free (even urged) to develop and change. I can't regret the approval which greeted my first three books of verse, because it fortified me during a couple of later decades in which I was dismissed by many as an irrelevant, foot-dragging formalist.

Some of the American poets of your generation were criticized for being too aware of Europe in their writing. What did Europe do for you as a young poet, do you think?

When my wife and I mentioned to her Uncle Hinkley that we were going to Rome on a fellowship, he said, 'Ever been to Minneapolis, Dick?' Well, I had been to Minneapolis, and to every other part of my country, which I love for its richness, variety, energy, and residual rawness. It seems to me that the United States, though not a coherent culture, is a sufficient one, and that Americans don't now need to cross the sea, like Henry James's heroines, in order to achieve fineness by looking at paintings in the Louvre. Yet precisely because of our present sufficiency, there is no need to choose between Minneapolis and Rome, and no reason why American art and consciousness shouldn't draw gratefully upon Europe and the whole of what used to be called the Western Tradition.

   In provincial societies, many writers and critics long for distinct national identity and style. So it was with us in the 19th century, and it was against such longing that Poe repeatedly said, 'The world at large is the proper stage for the literary histrio.' In 1999, that quarrel is over and done with. It seems that, without help or hindrance from critical leadership, American poetry has become unmistakably American, and that it can draw upon all times and places without ceasing to be ours. In a recently-exhumed lecture of the Fifties, Randall Jarrell said of American poets, 'We may seem to ourselves citizens of this world; to the world we seem inmates of our own States.' That's even truer now, forty-odd years later. I won't venture to say what our identifying signs are – the manhandling of forms? a sharp, unmellow, colloquial voice? an attraction to the concrete and the unpoetic? But in any case we are now recognizably American, and need not worry if, for instance, we are exhilarated and overpowered by the baroque architecture of Italy, as I once was and still am.

You were in residence at the American Academy in Rome during the mid-'50s, when Anthony Hecht was also there. Did you learn much from each other about poetry, form, method and what have you?

It was very good to coincide with Tony in Rome. I have always felt an affinity for his work, the existence of which has heartened me in my own, and in Rome and thereafter I've found him fine and often hilarious company. At the Academy, we showed each other our works-in-progress, and once gave a reading together in Yehudi Wyner's studio. He once told, at our dinner table, a joke about Vegetable Soup which was very long and full of 'meanwhiles', and so extremely funny that he couldn't finish it without falling from his chair and writhing on our faux-marble floor. I don't think we ever talked abstractly about 'form and method'. Tony's poetry discovers much that is cruel and painful in the world, and I have other emphases, but our practice and our implicit standards so agree that, had we cared for poetic gang-warfare, we might have found ourselves in the same gang.

Yours, his, was an angst-ridden generation of poets with more than its fair share of suicides and alcoholics. How did you manage to keep the balance that Clive James, for example, observed in you in the early '60s?

Like many of that generation, I liked to drink too much and be crazy. If I've lived to be a hale and moderate seventy-eight, I think it has much to do with my long, good marriage and my enjoyment of my children. If you like being a family man, it can keep you steady. Some of my contemporaries had the bad luck to be unstable not merely from drink but from innate psychological imbalance; I was spared that. Finally (though I make no claim to wisdom), I think that the diversity of my life has been good for me; I've written in many genres; I've done a lot of translation; I've taught school for thirty-six years; I've served as a town committeeman, a general editor, an academy president, and a lay reader; I've been a

Broadway lyricist; I've played a great deal of tennis and *bocce*; I've tramped, botanized, bicycled, and spaded my own gardens. When a poet-friend of ours committed suicide, Stanley Kunitz said, 'He was in the poetry prison' – meaning that our friend had spent too much time cooped up with his nerve-ridden brilliant poems, his books, his booze, and his devouring ambition.

Theodore Roethke refers to you as 'Dick' in one of his letters. He was a very different poet from you. How well did you know each other?

Back around 1950, my wife wrote Ted Roethke an appreciative note about a poem of his which had appeared in the *New Yorker*. He was so appreciative of the note that he at once came east from Seattle and paid us the first of many visits – appearing on our South Lincoln doorstep with a case of champagne and with a silver dollar for each of the children. He became our good and boisterous friend, and I saw him often, on both coasts. If he stayed with you, or you with him, the day began with whiskey sours, but fortunately he enjoyed sobering excursions – to the Seattle zoo, perhaps, or to our lawn for some savagely competitive games of *bocce*. He was a tall, heavy, groaning, delicate man. On the tennis court he had improbably light footwork and quick hands, getting everything back with excellent touch; and underneath the tough-guy or gangster manner which he often put on, there was a like delicacy of feeling. I recall his reading aloud Charlotte Mew's 'The Trees are Down' with great passion and with a nearly breaking voice.

Did you ever show each other your poems?

Yes, we did at times look at each other's new poems, and we kept up with each other's efforts as they came. I have a memory of being warmly pleased by his praise of my little poem 'Exeunt', and annoyed by his saying of 'The Undead' it was 'a little too much like Wystan'. When we talked of poets and poetry, he showed a constant devotion to Louise Bogan, Kunitz, and Auden.

He had this division between a kind of Yeatsian formalism – which you might have wished him to stick with while dropping the Yeats – and a sort of free-form near madness.

As he knew and said of himself, Ted was to some extent an un-jelled personality – I take that to be the theme of some of the 'Lost Son' poems, with their pattern of regression and reintegration. In consequence, he was vulnerable to influences: he took on something of Dylan Thomas's social behaviour, I think, and was obviously taken captive for a time by the cadences of Yeats.

You're quite right in saying that Roethke was very different from me and he was, indeed, very different from himself. Nevertheless we had respect and affection for each other, and for each other's talents. I don't think it would make any real sense for a critic, on the basis of Roethke's western-ness, mental breakdowns, and experiments with loose form, to put him and me into opposing categories.

Mariani's biography of Berryman records that you and Berryman once went together to get Delmore Schwartz released from the police-station after one of his drunken excesses. How well did you know these two? Did the Dream Songs *come as a shock? They seem to have shaken Lowell a bit.*

I never knew Schwartz very well, though he and I had served together on an NBA jury which gave the prize to Red Warren's *Brother to Dragons*, or perhaps to a book of Conrad Aiken's. And we'd once had an evening's rambling talk in Syracuse, admiring Socrates (as I remember) for drinking the hemlock rather than letting his friends spirit him away. On the occasion mentioned by Paul Mariani, Schwartz was in fact more mad than drunk, as the police knew by the time Berryman and I arrived at the station. He was shouting through the bars of his cell, 'Everything I do is done on the orders of the Chief Executive,' and the police, who didn't wish to cope with madness, were glad to let us pay his drunk-and-disorderly fine and take him away. From the early '60s on, Berryman and I were friends and, though we saw each other seldom, were in frequent touch by mail or telephone. John often called at the damnedest, darkest hours of the night. His successive book-manuscripts were sent me for criticism, as they were to Bill Meredith and a number of other friends. It troubled me to say – as I did – that the latter books, though full of fine flashes, were uneven and not up to the *Dream Songs*. He was generous toward my work, and it was at his urging that I got going on a translation of his favourite Molière play, *The School for Wives*.

I heard Geoffrey Hill, when asked at a poetry reading why he wrote such glum poems, reply, 'Because it pleases me to be gloomy.' Unusually, perhaps, for a poet of the twentieth century, you are not attracted by gloominess.

Well, gloom isn't very agreeable in everyday conversation, but I think that Geoffrey Hill is quite right to say that in poems it can be pleasing: Tennyson and Longfellow can be gloriously morose, and Auden tells the poet to 'Sing of human unsuccess / In a rapture of distress.' Affirmation and delight can also be pleasing in poems. Indeed, a lyric or song-like poem can satisfy by the strong, simple expression of any emotion whatever. But when poetry becomes more complex than a song, and offers more than a single mood or message, a good part of its power to please must lie in its articulation of a whole consciousness, with all its doubts, ignorances, shifts, and contradictions. Articulateness exalts us, regardless of what is said. I have an inclination to be positive, but I hope that in most of my work I'm not a cheerleader for the universe but a describer of how it feels to be in it.

Well, it's commonly said that happiness writes white. But at the back of your optimism and equability there seems to be some supporting kind of faith in an ultimately benign world. Could you say something that might confirm or qualify this impression?

I do have such a trust. Voltaire's *Candide*, with which I've had a long working acquaintance, argues rightly that it's inhuman to be sunny in the presence of agony and disaster. But to trust in the 'ultimately benign' nature of things is another matter. I should add that, though I once experienced a severe depression through the unwitting over-use of valium, it's my nature to be of good cheer.

I suppose a poem like 'Children of Darkness' suggests a kind of faith in the ultimate goodness of the world:

> Gargoyles is what they are at worst, and should
> They preen themselves
> On being demons, ghouls or elves,
> The holy chiaroscuro of the wood
> Still would embrace them. They are good.

One can see how a conservationist or evolutionist might think these fungi and whatnot are good in that they fill an essential role in the cycle of things, but you mean to imply more than that?

Yes, the poem is about fungi, and their bad reputation in folklore, and the good work that they do in the renovation of nature. At the same time, it may be read as a brisk, oblique, forty-five line statement of what Milton more grandly argues in *Paradise Lost*: that, in the great rhythms of the creation, good is brought out of evil.

An unattuned British ear might feel that it neatly expresses an intellectual or even religious idea but, to put it oddly, it doesn't feel as if you felt it on the pulses, to adapt Keats. This is a type of criticism I am sure you have encountered before, and not just from the 'wilder' end of the po-

etic world: Jarrell wrote: 'In Wilbur the man who produces the poems is somehow impersonal and anonymous.'

If I have your permission to be a little hazy, let me begin by saying that many people, just after World War II, experienced that shaken sense of meaning and purpose which led, in France, to existentialist philosophy and the lonely, depleted figures of Giacometti. In such an atmosphere, there could be a special charge on any writing which tried to be passionately faithful to things, to external reality. A poem of that kind could offer not merely the capture of something in words, but a sense of escaping from the isolate ego in the direction of 'the other', and ultimately, perhaps, toward a more intelligible human world. Back in 1948, after a poetry conference at Bard College, I said that sort of thing at length in an essay awkwardly called 'The Bottles Become New, Too', in which I responded to the conference speeches of Louise Bogan and William Carlos Williams; Bill Williams was one poet in whom I found the kind of drama I'm talking about: in a poem like 'Young Sycamore', he's on-stage only in the first line, where he says 'I must tell you'; the rest of the poem – what he urgently wants to say – is wholly concerned with conveying the upward sweep and ramification of a small street-side tree, from sidewalk-level to the tip of its crown. Williams is full of poems in which he breaks out of himself and makes implicitly ecstatic contact with some part of reality; a few pieces of broken glass in the gravel can suffice him. I found, in my early days, a related quality in Marianne Moore's descriptive coups, in those poems where Lawrence outwitted the 'obscene ego', and in the Francis Ponge who wrote *Le Parti Pris des Choses*.

All that may begin to explain why one of my earliest poems says 'have objects speak', and praises 'the devout intransitive eye' of Pieter de Hooch. Rightly or wrongly, I felt back then that it could be downright good to seem anonymous, and to let much of one's notions and emotions be implicit – as, for instance, in Williams' little poem 'Between Walls'. I was encouraged in this, no doubt, by Eliot's recommendation of impersonality, by my own reserve, and by my dislike of lapel-grabbing persons and poems.

How well did you know James Dickey? He's a strange poet, but, in a poem entitled 'To Richard Wilbur' he puts the distinction – wild versus cultivated, personal versus impersonal – as between you and himself – perhaps more skilfully than I have just attempted:

>   I sit
> In the American night, and, through you, remember
> That the great wild thing is not seeing
> All the way in to the center,

> But holding yourself at the edge,
> Alive, where one can get a look.

Does that seem a clearer way of getting at it?

I'm touched to learn that Jim Dickey wrote a poem to me, and distressed that I can't at the moment locate it in my library.

It's in T*he Whole Motion.*

I don't get a clear sense, from the lines quoted, of where he is placing me. Jim was famously inconsistent: he often praised me, and as often did not, but he never gave me any wilder-than-thou nonsense. We were lucky, at the Wesleyan Press, to recruit him toward the start of our venture, and to publish the several books which were his best work. I liked his vision and daring; my chief reservation about his work was that he sometimes confused imagination with the supposition of impossibilities. His introduction to a *Selected Poems* of E. A. Robinson was admirable.

It's an orthodoxy of our day, the idea of the poet as central in the poem, the Berrymans and Lowells, say. But Yeats called that sort of thing 'the cult of sincerity' and he was echoed in this by Geoffrey Hill who, notwithstanding Mercian Hymns, *and until very recently, preferred to eschew anything that smacked of the autobiographical. (Whitman declared 'I am many'.) But, curiously, while you must believe in some sort of distancing, your poems have a kind of Wilbur aura. Personality in poetry doesn't have to be loudmouthed. Would you say that a change came about in your attitude to distance, impersonality, as you moved to a plainer style?*

Lowell had a great talent, and in any style he was bound to be of the greatest interest. The best of Berryman's *Dream Songs* are coruscating. Though they take place in the small theatre of subjective frenzy, Sylvia Plath's later poems are frequently stunning. Yet I don't think that the autobiographical movement turned out to be, as Cal put it in 1960, a 'breakthrough back into life' for American poetry. The standard awful poem of the past forty years has been a sort of artless diary entry in free verse. And even among the gifted, the mode has had its disadvantages. Though the central and literal I of the poem may have wide-ranging table talk, the world of the poem is a diminished one. A certain amount of self-dramatisation and grandiosity are inevitable, and at worst the autobiographical poem can modulate into celebrity gossip.

I have of, course, written some poems, early and late – 'The Pardon' for instance, or the recent poem 'This Pleasing Anxious Being' – which are taken straight out of my life, and in which, I, or the person I was, is central. You're right in saying that I've grown a bit more willing to be plain and personal, and though I've never focused on projecting a personality, I'm glad the poems sound like somebody. What Emerson said – that the deeper we go into ourselves, the more we are like everyone else – has always seemed to me true, and I hope that the 'I' of my poems is one that any reader can enter into. There's a habitable 'I', I think, in the last stanza of 'Mayflies', which is the title poem of my forthcoming book:

> Watching those lifelong dancers of a day
> As night closed in, I felt myself alone
>   In a life too much my own,
> More mortal in my separateness than they –
> Unless, I thought, I had been called to be
>   Not fly or star
> But one whose task is joyfully to see
> How fair the fiats of the caller are.

That has my feelings in it, and can rightly be read as the thoughts of a poet who is recognizing his vocation; but any reader will have felt the loneliness of the human individual, and wondered about the use of consciousness in our cosmos.

Maybe that remark of Jarrell's, about your impersonality and anonymity – it was made at a time when a much more aggressive 'I' was in fashion – connects with the distinction slipped into your last remark, 'the thoughts of a poet' as against 'any reader will have felt ...'
   You try to identify your position as a poet in 'Cottage Street, 1953' by contrast with Sylvia Plath's deadly brilliance. The poem has been quoted and discussed, almost as an exemplar, by Carol Simpson Stern in her piece on your work in Contemporary Poets. *The poem closes, contrasting the young suicide with the aged Edna Ward's eighty-eight summers of grace and love, with:*

> ... Sylvia, who, condemned to live,
> Shall study for a decade, as she must,
> To state at last her brilliant negative
> In poems free and helpless and unjust.

But Edna Ward, so far as I know, was not an ocean-going poet, like Berryman and Plath, to name but two, and the options for poets seem to be harder. In your Shenandoah *piece, you speak of community and suggest a poet should maintain a sort of not-alienated but ongoing quarrel with his culture. Yet you also speak of poems as 'autonomous'. This suggests a bit of a conundrum since the conscious intellect is not the gatherer of the material that arrives for the poet and hardly the director of where it goes. How can we fit the two together?*

In writing that poem, I had no idea how incendiary it might prove to mention Sylvia Plath. What I sought to do was to remember an awkward and poignant occasion, and to describe it with an equitable sympathy for all concerned. Most people have taken it that way, but I have been charged by a few critics with such things as anti-feminism, anti-confessionalism, envy, or a complacent shallowness. Having been so disagreeably misunderstood, I was grateful to Ted Hughes for saying, in a letter of 1995, 'Your poem about meeting S.P. is to my mind the single truest best thing about her, the best most accurate page'.

I didn't think of 'Cottage Street, 1953' as arguing a poetic position – certainly not an anti-Plath position; but it does take for granted that a poetry of troubled self-expression is a limited poetry, and it regrets that a brilliant but 'helpless' talent could not live to embody more of life.

It's presumptuous and vain, as you imply, to say what poetry 'should' do, and even if some inspired gasbag were to come up with perfect desiderata, poets couldn't force themselves to comply with them. We write what we can. At the same time, we're not Aeolian harps; with luck, we have as persons some management of our hearts and minds, some willing involvements with people and culture, and those things affect our poems. We're also consentingly guided – though tastes differ – by our sense of what, in the poetry of the past, has helped us as persons to live and to know.

Yeats once criticized a poet contemporary for lacking chaos; and Plato pointed out that, when it came to poetry, sane men were outstripped by madmen and fools. Does this ever give you cause or pause for doubt?

Insanity can seem pretty exciting when viewed from the outside, but to the insane it's a cramped, repetitive, self-bound condition: a mentally afflicted friend told me, when I visited him in an asylum, that he no longer read the papers because they were always about *him*. When poets speak favourably of craziness and folly, as we all do, they're speaking of imagination and of all the other-than-rational means by which poetry proceeds and persuades. They're also thinking of how the best, freshest poems often happen when, not knowing quite where their words are headed, they trust intuition and inspiration to discover what they mean to say. I guess I was partly thinking of such experiences when I said, in 'Walking to Sleep',

> Step off assuredly into the blank of your mind.

Something will come to you.

Yeats was a calculating poet who needed a system to hang his poems on, and it might seem odd for him to be recommending the chaotic; but he knew so much about the diverse human heart, and how to dramatize it, that his poems are full of the unexpected. I forget the butt and context of his remark, but I dare say he was criticizing someone for his want of the unexpected – for his tidy predictability and foregone conclusions. Strangely enough, predictability is often the fault of poets thought to be wild; I like some of Allen Ginsberg's early lines very well, but taken in quantity his poems have a stillborn quality. Too often you know what he is going to say, and in what manner.

Alan Williamson, in his book of critical essays, Eloquence and Mere Life, *remarked: 'The generation of Wilbur gave metre a bad name largely because it did not do much with metre that had not already been done by Auden, Stevens or Ransom.' These three are a curious line-up – no Frost for one thing. Yet it is surprising that while you have invented some interesting stanzaic forms, you have also stuck fairly rigidly to traditional rhyme, with a bit of half-rhyme, eye-rhyme, here and there. Auden did develop new types of rhyming technique – as did MacNeice and Dylan Thomas, of course – but experiment doesn't seem to have attracted you so much, despite a couple of pieces in Anglo-Saxon metrics.*

The word 'experiment' always introduces an element of stupor into any conversation about poetry, because it seems impossible for us to get rid of the idea that technical innovation resembles scientific discovery, and involves some sort of progress, in the light of which some are stragglers and others in the vanguard. It's a long time since there were theories and manifestos about how free verse should be done, and for most of America's myriad free-versers the sole remaining technical consideration is where to put the line-breaks; yet every damned one of them thinks that he is experimental because it was anciently proclaimed that forward-looking poetry was going to dispense with metre and rhyme. What dreary rot. There can be, and are, good free verse poems, but significant chance-taking in poetry is not a matter of form alone but of a concerting of thought, tone, diction, sound, cadence and all else that goes into a poem's making.

I don't think that metres and stanza-forms and rhyme-systems, as we find them described in poetry handbooks, are very stimulating in themselves, whether the tricks are new or old; it's the great embodiments that matter, and those don't come along in generational increments. I don't believe that I've ever been inspired by anyone's mere technique, or been moved to be a technical show-off like Austin Dobson; what moves me is the fusion of speech and measure in Frost, and the fusion of that with what is spoken; what moves me is the way that a passionate argument, in Milton, can turn the sonnet into a cataract. Argument comes first always, as so many have said before me, and form is of value in proportion as it empowers the argument.

As you've noted, a good many of my poems – starting as early as 'Mined Country' – have invented stanza-structures, and I recall that when I published 'All These Birds' in the *New Yorker,* Elizabeth Drew wrote me to say (amusedly) that I had carried baroque invention about as far as she thought necessary. Some critics, I suppose, don't recognize my sort of inventiveness because it is axiomatic with them that metre and rhyme are intrinsically retrograde. Well, in any case I have made up a lot of stanzas, not for decoration or ostentation but because each seemed to me organically expressive of something I was striving to utter. That sort of one-time venture cannot, of course, be replicated like a football play or scientific experiment, but my luckier efforts might encourage a young poet to feel that a poem can sometimes find its unique, specific form. I'm inclined to think that Coventry Patmore does that in his 'Magna Est Veritas'.

Yes, George Herbert, not known for ostentatious experiment, has a higher proportion of invented stanza-forms in his total output than many other poets, and most 'experimenters', that I can think of. But it's fairly clear that Owen thought his message on war would be served well by his development of pararhymes or half-rhymes.

I haven't been drawn to half-rhyme or off-rhyme, though Auden was surely successful with it, because it's very hard to sustain a consistent degree of off-ness. Lacking such consistency, the rhyme can seem intermittent; or it can seem inappropriately tricky, as in Wilfred Owen's 'Strange Meeting'.

That's a pretty early example of that type of rhyme, of course. But it surprises me that a good rhymer like you should find half-rhyme any harder than the old rhymes. Less satisfying temperamentally, I could understand.

I expect you're right – that I'm not strongly attracted to using off-rhymes, and haven't done much pondering of the question. I've heard that Auden, in his notebooks, made for his own use a dictionary of off-rhymes: since a master technician like Auden did that in order to be subtly and evenly 'off', and would never have needed a personal dictionary of pure rhymes, I think there's some reason to feel that good off-rhyming is harder to do than the pure thing.

Oh, Auden, I thought he was an absolute magpie of dictionaries. Maybe when he started there were no off-rhyme ones to acquire.

No doubt long practice would make it easier. Emily Dickinson used more and more off-rhyme as she went along, and came to feel that 'tree' and 'sky', and 'man' and 'tongue', are rhymes. I'll swallow that along with her other idiosyncrasies, because she can be marvellous, but I should hate to see her rhyming imitated by the less inspired.

Too late, I'm afraid: it's all over the place – at least this side of the language.

There is, in fact, one form of my invention which I have used three times – in 'Thyme Flowering among Rocks', 'Zea', and 'Signatures' – and which I believe some other poets have found useful. It employs the haiku as its stanza-form, and in each stanza rhymes the first and third lines, as some translators of individual haiku (Blunden, Henderson) have done in the past. I like the form, when I have a subject which seems to demand it; it calls for a strong flow of speech-rhythm, yet there are cross-effects of the quantitative, and that makes for interesting texture.

A decade or so back someone over here published – fairly fugitively – a sort of epic called 'The Matter of Britain' using such a stanza without rhyme as the staple measure. I don't know if your example had encouraged him. But enough, for the moment, on technique.
　　You were a cultural exchange representative to the former USSR during 1961. What sort of brief for the visit did you have? How deeply did the visit affect you? For example, did it make you more, or less, scared when the Cuban Missile Crisis developed?

Peter Viereck and I, constituting a two-man literary delegation, were sent over to the USSR as part of an exchange programme designed to create, despite political tensions, some measure of good will and understanding. On the day before our departure, Peter and I were consulting in the White House with our friend Arthur Schlesinger, a recent visitor to Russia, when a secretary hurried in with the news that Moscow had resumed the atmospheric testing of nuclear weapons. That was not auspicious, and it did affect the tone of our several weeks' visit; yet we were well and cordially treated by our hosts at the Moscow Writers' Union. We asked them if we could meet Russian writers not at banquets full of toasts to world peace, but quietly in ones and twos, and they obliged us. Of a longish list of names we gave them, they arranged quiet meetings with all but two, one of whom (Akhmatova) was in hospital, and one of whom, I fear, was being cured of political dissent in a madhouse. Our first encounter was a two-hour tea with Ilya Ehrenburg in his dacha where, underneath a Modigliani portrait of Akhmatova, we talked in French so as to tease our interpreter (and Party watchdog) who didn't have that language. It was Ehrenburg who initiated the teasing, and who surprised us a bit by his liberal criticism of all that, in Soviet life, conspired to infantilize the people and deprive them of knowledge and initiative. *Pravda*, he said, should start printing the truth. At the same time, Ehrenburg was absolute in his support of Krushchev's bristling foreign policy...

Well, I must stop or you will be sorry that you asked the question. It was a fascinating visit, and not all the talk was of politics, and in a person-to-person sense our good will mission was a success. We met with many such lively people as the novelist Leonov, the brilliant translator Andrei Sergeiev, and (in Tbilisi) the affable poet Joseph Noneshvili. I've been back just once. In 1990 or so, just when Yeltsin was coming to power, my wife and I flew to Moscow where John Ashbery and I were to give a reading at the Mayakovsky Museum, where my wife hoped to view the scene of Natasha's first ball, and where we all would have luncheon at the Voznesenskys' in Peredelkino. We were met at the plane by several young writers who conveyed excitement and hope at emerging from what one of them called seventy years of repression and falsehood. With them was an older woman who had been my hostess (and watchdog) thirty years before, and who now had tears in her eyes as she lamented the collapse of a Socialist dream for which millions had died. In contrast to that young hope, and to that grieving idealism, we soon after chanced to meet in a restaurant some young men of a type then emerging – empty young entrepreneurs, sniggeringly cynical, who in their greed for money regarded themselves, I fear, as just like Americans.

Clive James, reviewing Walking to Sleep, *spoke of you at an American Embassy reading as 'Wilbur, the epitome of cool. It was all there: the Ivy League haircut, the candy-stripe jacket, the full burnished image of the Amherst phi bete. ... he took European Culture out of his pocket and laid it right on us. We were stoned. It was the Kennedy era and somehow it seemed plausible that the traditional high culture of Europe should be represented in a super-refined form by an American who looked like a jet-jockey and that the State Department should pay the hotel bills.' James seems to have been intending to link the success of your poetry with the optimism of the Kennedy period. Do you think there was a link? Did you notice a gradual change in approval, coverage, after the tragic ending of those hopes?*

I am stoned by Clive James's account of my appearance, or apparition, at the Embassy. I recall the occasion quite well. I began my reading with some poems by other Americans, the first being Elizabeth Bishop's 'Over 2000 Illustrations and a Complete Concordance'. (Elizabeth, it turned out, was in the audience.) Then I read one of those 'dream songs' which John Berryman had lately unveiled at a poetry conference in Washington, and followed with Jim Cunningham's exquisite poem 'To the Reader'. After the reading there was sherry and a number of pleasant encounters; I was particularly glad to meet the poet and Milton scholar F.T. Prince.

Naturally I didn't regard myself as a Kennedy-era phenomenon. I wasn't really, having been around for some time.

I didn't intend to suggest you were such a passing phenomenon but that perhaps there might have been a timely coincidence of the Kennedys, the mood of the period, and the tenor of your work at that stage. Sorry to interrupt.

However, I think that all American writers and artists – and especially Norman Mailer, who wrote and spoke volumes on the subject – felt that the presence in the White House of a couple who valued arts and letters conferred upon them (the writers and artists) something like full citizenship. That was exhilarating. Prior to the Kennedys, I had always found Washington, for all its wondrous museums and libraries, a sort of Brasilia, a government town where politics was after all the only serious subject. No doubt the taste and culture of the Kennedys has been exaggerated, but the fact is that their brief tenure began what is still going on, an increased celebration and sponsorship of the arts and humanities at the national level. When Lyndon Johnson was inaugurated in 1965, Roger Stevens ushered my wife and me into a 'bus together with Erich Leinsdorf, Maria Tallchief, Paul Horgan, Reuben Mamoulian, De Snodgrass, Adolph Green, Edward Durrell Stone, and many others. Off we roared across Washington toward our reserved section at the ceremony, a motorcycle escort leading us through all the red lights, our bus bearing a placard with the glorious and comical legend, CULTURAL LEADERS.

When Lowell reviewed Berryman's 77 Dream Songs, *he spoke of a 'hazardous, imperfect book ... the threat of mannerism, and worse, disintegration.' Rather later, though, he came to think he'd been wrong: 'I misjudged them, and was rattled by their mannerism.' Some have suggested that Lowell's* Notebook *was indebted to the* Dream Songs. *Whether that's true or not, both poets latched on to the idea of the sequence, and made use of a sort of elastic form to try to prefabricate a long poem. You were never really tempted by either example to go for the huge poem or sequence, were you? Was it their example that 'saved' you, or were there other considerations?*

According to the Library of Congress transcript of the Tuesday afternoon session of the 1962 National Poetry Festival, Roy Basler began by saying, 'Mr Robert Lowell, we regret to say, cannot be with us,' and proceeded to introduce John Berryman, who read for the first time 'Filling her compact & delicious body' and other sections of 'a poem in progress'. Nevertheless, I'm almost certain that Cal was there, and I have a mental picture of him and me urging John to pull his new poems together and make a book of them. Be that as it may, what's certain is that Berryman's *Dream Songs* prompted Lowell to find a comparable catch-all form in which to be offhand, spontaneous, fragmentary, and additive.

I've never read all of Lowell's unrhymed sonnets or Berryman's triple sestets, because those accumulations are too dense and demanding to be experienced as long poems; but I've found wonderful work in both, especially the latter. And while I am confessing, I may as well own that I have never sat down and read doggedly through the *Sandover* sequence of my friend Jimmy Merrill; what I do is to make occasional raids upon it, and carry off what delights me. It's not that I am lazy: when I read as a critic and scholar, who has some insights and wants to test them fully, I can consume all of Disraeli's novels or ponder every last verse and sentence of Poe. But when I am a poet reading poems, it is a slow, intense business that has nothing to do with covering ground.

Getting around to your final question there, Robert Frost once electrified an audience at Bread Loaf by giving a talk entitled 'The Dullness of Wordsworth'. What he turned out to mean was that Wordsworth had an admirable ability to write plain, low-keyed passages between his moments of lyric elevation – an essential ability, I should think, if one is going to compose readable poems of great length. Actually, Frost himself was seldom as flat (and never as long) as Wordsworth could be; and as for me, I seem to have no gift for writing connective material. Though I strive not to be laboured, I am a terribly slow writer who will not go on to line six unless line five strikes him as in some way exciting. That means that my kind of long poem – 'The Mind-Reader', for instance, which took me months to write – will be a hundred and forty-odd lines at most.

Another reason for my not working in great suites and sequences (though I respect the capability in others) is the fact that, as I've said elsewhere, what I try to do in any poem is to use up my present awareness of the subject. Coming to the end of a poem, I don't feel impelled to say 'but' or 'furthermore', because the buts and furthermores are already there in what I have written.

Perhaps I have taken care of the huge poem impulse by doing rather mammoth jobs of translation: I have just finished rendering in couplets the 2,068 lines of Molière's first verse comedy *The Bungler*.

Reading the letters and lives of your poet contemporaries – people such as Berryman, Jarrell, Lowell and Roethke, to stick with the safely dead – a British reader might be forgiven for detecting a paradox. The poets sometimes seem to despise the general culture's attitude to poetry, art, and themselves, and yet to be almost commercially competitive and jealous of each other when it comes to the awards and prizes conferred by that very culture. In short, they seem to exhibit all the drives for success and status that in other areas they have often deprecated in the culture. Is this a mistaken impression, do you think? If not, how can they have it both ways? Is it a basic fear that the literary culture is short-lived now and not permanent or as on-going as it always was?

I don't think that your paradoxical impression is wholly correct, though there's truth in it. American writers have their moments of exasperation with the general culture, because if there is a new crassness in the world it will often make its first appearance in our innovative country, promising to endanger all custom, cultivation, and respect. Yet there is a limit to our self-dislike, and I remember enjoying it when Mary McCarthy, in spirited response to some French person's remarks on American materialism, observed that misers, though common in certain countries, are very rare in the United States. A half-century ago, I was a participant in the Harvard conference to which Randall Jarrell read his celebrated lecture on 'The Obscurity of the Poet'. The piece was full of Randall's customary wit, and initially it gave visible pleasure to the audience and to those seated on the stage – Tate, Ransom, Marianne Moore, Lowell, Kenneth Burke, Pierre Emmanuel, and many others. Before it was over, however, the lecture had gone on a little too long about the public's consumerism, its interest in washing-machines, its lapsed literacy, its neglect of poetry and all the arts. Stephen Spender, rising to comment, spoke for some of the Americans present when he asked whether one really wanted to live in a society of bluestockings and high-art groupies.

What I am saying is that most American artists are of two minds about these matters – prepared to deplore Disney, squalling rock-bands, Wal-Mart, fast food, and the commercial rat-race, yet glad of the nation's vitality, its human diversity, and its undoubted cultural vigour. Last month I had a two-hour major operation, in the midst of which I hazily awoke to find that the anaesthetist was asking me questions about one of my early poems. That was quite a surprise. The questions were sensitive and intelligent, and so I was gratified; but if he had not known my poems, I would not have thought it an indictment of our culture.

The first three of the poets you mention were indeed concerned with status. Roethke and Lowell were lifelong rankers. When I first knew them, each liked to discuss with me the pecking order of the 'younger poets', usually managing to assign the other to third place. It was the one slightly tiresome thing about their conversation. Berryman, as his poems witness, was much interested in fame and was dismissive of all but an admired elect among his contemporaries. Once, when I told him of my participation, together with some fine writers and editors, in a memorial tribute to Louise Bogan, he outrageously said, 'You're consorting with your inferiors, pal.' But it must be stated about these three poets that their talents were large and genuine, that they aspired more to Parnassus than to prizes, and that, for all their daft ambition, they did not grossly market themselves. I can think of only a few poets, and those not of our best, who have been commercially aggressive in the Andy Warhol manner – forever promoting, doing what will get publicity, haunting the media. Though all poets, I'm sure, inwardly glory in their best work and hope for no end of recognition, it strikes me that by and large, even in this huckstering nation, the members of my profession are civil, generous, and comradely with one another.

My impressions come from the printed records. For example, Mary Jarrell's account of the 1962 National Poetry Festival – it's set out in her edition of her husband's letters – doesn't give an impression of full harmony, sweetness and light (though the Cuban crisis may have to take some of the blame).

But back to poetry itself. You remarked earlier that you write very slowly but do not produce version after version. Do you carry the poem around in your head till, as Yeats – another slow worker – has it, the last thing clicks into place like a box snapping closed? At which point you reach for the typewriter?

I wish that I could quickly sketch a first draft, as Keats could, and then go back and fill up the holes; or that I could come home from a woods ramble, as Housman could, with a whole poem sounding in my head. Something dooms me to work alluvially, with pencil and paper, getting the first line just right and then undertaking the second. Unless I've foreseen that the poem will use some received pattern, my first few lines will decide for me, through their mood and phrasing and incipient argument, all matters of form: what the measures will be, and whether or not there are to be rhyme and stanza.

For anyone who writes as slowly as I, revision is something that happens not afterward but in transit, and I must be constantly alert to preserve the rhythms of offhand, natural speech. By the time I come to the end of a poem, I have so honed and worried it that it usually seems to be publishable, though I have of course suppressed a number of efforts wholly or in part: 'Parable' and 'On Having Misidentified a Wild Flower' were chopped off the ends of poems I had to discard.

A typewriter – even my old L.C. Smith – gives words something like the authority of print, and for fear of being falsely impressed I never touch the typewriter keys until my lines can convince me in pencil.

Auden wrote somewhere that there was nothing like copying out a poem in your own handwriting to get at the nub of the thing, all its dodges and shifts.

Eliot speaks of a poem often beginning as an almost wordless rhythm. Others report that a poem can begin almost as a dictated stanza shape; or may turn up as a more or less complete sonnet. Does this sort of thing happen to you on occasion?

I seldom write a sonnet, or a rondeau, or anything of that sort, but I have an inward sense of them and can tell – let's say, by the second line of an initial scrawl – when my emerging thought wants to animate such a skeleton. It's like the tennis player's ingrained knowledge of when and how to make a drop shot.

But how does the initial whisper of a poem in the imagination know that such a form exists? Isn't there a danger of conscious 'shaping' intervening too early?

Since you yourself have written sonnets – indeed a whole sequence of them – you'll readily guess my answer to that question. There may now be young American poets or 'creative writers' who read only contemporary verse but in my generation we all had an amateur's acquaintance with the whole body of English-language poetry. That meant that we'd read hundreds of sonnets, and memorized a few, and had come to know what sorts of argument can use to advantage one of the several versions of the form.

In The Formalist, *writing on 'Traditional Verse Forms', you remark: 'Robert Frost once said something like this: that if you feel like saying something for about eight lines, and then qualifying or unsaying it for six lines or so, you are probably about to write a Petrarchan sonnet. That is the way it should happen: the beginning poem, as it materializes, should choose that form whose logic will provide it with precision, economy and power.' Anthony Hecht has quibbled over that 'should' with you and Frost, suggesting that it is too prescriptive. On the surface, one would have expected you and Hecht largely to agree, since your formal concerns seem pretty close in some respects. But there's a sense in which all forms at some point become self-prescriptive: once you've chosen one, or it has chosen your incipient poem, you are committed to get it right. But Hecht makes a distinction in formal matters between what might be thought the simpler traditional forms, like quatrains and sonnets, and more complex types like sestinas, single and double canzones, villanelles and so forth. He speaks of properly preparing to use a complex form. I'm not sure that you have often tried these over-elaborate forms but I can't imagine from your poetics that you would 'prepare' a form, complex or otherwise, nor 'prepare' to use one.*

I couldn't possibly prepare to use a form. My experience in writing is far too passive for that: poems come to me, and I execute them, as best I can, in the manner which they seem to require. If I were to write a canzone, it would not be a deliberate project but a hunch or sudden impulse, triggered by the onset of some idea which called for the great stanza divisa of Spenser and Milton. Verse-writing students in America are often asked by their instructors, I can't imagine why, to try their hands at a sestina. Often those hands have not mastered any technique whatever, yet they're invited to take on an intricate form, which, unless done with much artifice and true motivation, is tedious and infuriating. What I mean by 'true motivation' is this: if one is going to repeat six end-words seven times in an interweaving fashion, the poem should have a state of mind – obsession, stunned incredulity, gloating insistence, or the like – which makes repetition dramatically probable. No doubt there is some other excuse for the sestina which I haven't yet thought of, but in any case it needs an excuse.

Well, there's hypnosis or sedation, I should think. Perhaps that's why the sestina's popular in creative writing classes.
  Do you occasionally feel uneasy with a poem 'finished' in one form and grow to feel you have to recast it in another?

To be sure, I've made some false starts; but I have never, I think, finished a poem in one form only to feel that I'd been Procrustean and must rework the material in another.

Over here, and I am sure in America, it has been polemically claimed that formal verse is necessarily right-wing. Why this should be so is left mysterious, and how the likes of Pound, Eliot, Jeffers and Hughes – who do not seem strikingly left-wing as free-versers – are supposed to fit in, I don't know, but have you met this prejudice?

Some years ago, in a foreword to a book called *Strong Measures*, I recalled how politicized the art of landscape gardening was in late eighteenth and early nineteenth century Europe. There was a universal association of formal regularity with authoritarian rule, and the 'picturesque' with untamed freedom. But that sort of clear, conscious connection between art and politics is rare. I think I remember that, during my youth, there was an irate organization called The League for Sanity in Poetry, which associated metre and rhyme with moral soundness and good order; they were crazy, of course, and if they had really read the poetry of their time they'd have seen – as I said in my little foreword – that a generous-spirited populism was equally well served by Sandburg's free verse and Lindsay's rollicking metres. There are political inferences to be drawn from most poetry, even from poems not overtly political, but at present it's a crude error to see politics in the mere choice between formal verse and free.

Formal verse might be an excuse to introduce the topic of translation. You are one of a number of translators who moved verse translation away from the Poundian end of the seesaw and back to a sort of literal/literary formal accuracy. But Pound had cleared a path away from what might be called translatorese and even formalists benefited, don't you think?

Ezra Pound's rendering of Voltaire's poem to Madame du Châtelet ('Si vous voulez que j'aime encore') is a lively Imagist exercise, in which he turns all of the original's abstract words into concrete things; but among its infidelities to Voltaire is its suppression of the poem's warm and touching final evocation of Friendship. When I mentioned this to a scholar and devotee of Pound, he said, 'Oh well, at the time he did that translation, Pound was in a depressed and cynical mood.' Which made me want to explode and say, 'Oh, poor Mr Pound, are you in a mood? Do go and botch somebody else's poem, and then you'll feel better.' One reason I can be inflammable in this connection is that one of my most fortunate and accurate translations is of the Voltaire poem in question. However, I must say in fairness that Pound was not pretending to translate strictly; his version was one of two free-verse pieces collectively entitled, as I remember, 'Impressions of François-Marie Arouet'.

Pound's impressions and adaptations led to the 'imitations' of Lowell, which for all their merit were sometimes cavalier, and his urging that we 'make it new' has prompted the too-clever 'updating' of some classic plays. But I think you are quite right about his largely beneficial influence on translation. He set the example of summoning China and Provence, Cavalcanti and Propertius, in distinguished and striking language, and after him a pedestrian dictionary fidelity could no longer suffice.

In your translation work you have again concentrated on what one might briefly characterize as formal perfectionists – La Fontaine, Molière, Racine, Valéry – who might be close to you in mind-set, or imagination-

set. Some theorists think this a required and essential match for good translators whereas others suggest that opposites might be equally effective. One is often surprised at what Lowell attempted – and, admittedly, some of the messes he made. Did you select authors from whom you hoped to learn for your own work or those with whom you thought half the battle was done because of shared drives or temperament?

Your old friend, William Jay Smith, believes that an affinity is essential between translator and translated, and he must be temperamentally very different from you in that he has concentrated on Laforgue. But you have translated only a few ballades of Villon. You left most of him alone. Was this a question of affinities? He is in some ways a gift to translator-poets in that his opus is very small.

Bill Smith's happy affinity for Laforgue has most recently produced a delightful prose memoir of Laforgue's days in Berlin. I do think that if one is going to translate any author in quantity and over a period of many years, one had better feel singularly attuned to his mind and heart. I feel so about Molière, whom I've been putting into English verse since 1952. Of course, there are reasons other than strong affinity for deciding to do this or that job of translation. I much admire Racine's psychological speed and accuracy, and the powerful changes he plays upon a small vocabulary; but his Jansenist vision is repugnant to me, and I think that what determined me to take on the *Andromaque* anyway was that my particular knacks and experience made me (so I thought) the right person to risk it. There was also the fact that I was being strongly urged to do it by friends in the academy and the theatre.

One quite secondary motive for translating drama is that it can unlimber the tongue, and give one practice in tones of voice which one's own poems haven't yet employed. Something like that was part of my attraction to Villon; he offered an opportunity for enlarging imposture. Back in the mid-1960s, when I was a fellow at Wesleyan's Center for the Humanities, I had a notion to make an anthology of the best Englishings of Villon's ballades – some of which I thought I might represent by a *concours* of rival translations. The project was never completed, but it did lead me to do four of the ballades.

Shakespeare was clearly right, when it comes to pure rhyme, in reducing the quadruplet rhyme requirements of the sonnet in English to just pairs. You are a master of the couplet. I wonder if the quadruplet requirements of the ballade stanza played a part in edging you away from Villon?

It was never my idea to translate Villon in toto, and of course the extreme difficulty of the ballade form, in our rhyme-poor language, would have been dissuasive had the idea occurred to me. The translator of Villon is obliged to preserve the ballade form, because the form is part of the meaning: the ballade is above all suited to catalogue, to lists of things which can be collectively treated by the refrain, and its repetitions of rhyme and refrain are the music of similarity and ironic difference. Through keeping the form, one may get into small local difficulties with the content, as I did with the ballade about dead ladies.

This will indeed be the pot calling the kettle black, but I'm puzzled by some of your decisions in the 'Ballade of the Ladies of Time Past'. 'Shorn' – so close to 'tonsured' – seems a strange equivalent for 'chastré'. And I'm puzzled why Bertha has grown uniformly big with her feet, not to mention the arrival of the traitor Burgundy.

It was too bad that 'Berthe aux grands pieds' (who was Charlemagne's mother, I believe) couldn't fit her big feet into my tetrameter. My two lines about 'Jehanne' are true, and are true to Villon's feelings about her, but they do trade Lorraine for Burgundy, and they foresee a canonization which didn't take place until 1920. My use of 'shorn' assumes a knowledge of Abelard's story, and perhaps I should have found a blunter word. I think that the translation is generally successful, and that it's crucially faithful to the poem's several tones, but I'll grant that it takes slight liberties of a kind that I don't like to take, and that I've never allowed myself in doing Molière or Racine.

It's clear that a formal translator is sometimes painted into a corner by his source and the difficulty of transfer between languages. Extrication measures sometimes have to be taken, rhythmical and rhyming often in the first instance, but more complex ones in coping with word-play and cultural reference and so forth. And it's clear that the goal-posts move between doing a short one-off and a larger work. What, in general, has been your approach to these problems?

My general position is that any translator unwilling to be slavish is in the wrong racket. The challenge is to be stunningly slavish.

One can always quibble about something in a translation, as we both know. But your translations of Racine's Andromaque *and Molière's* Tartuffe *and other plays read extremely well. There's little tradition of acting and speaking of plays from the French classics among English-speaking acting companies. The dramatic couplet particularly is often seen as an alien vehicle for drama. (Some of even Shakespeare's couplet sequences sound dreadful.) Did you find that actors had problems in speaking your lines dramatically?*

I remember Tony Guthrie's telling me in 1955, when he was directing our musical *Candide*, that the English resist rhyming verse on stage because they associate it with 'panto' – with children's theatre. Nevertheless, Tony not long afterward directed Gielgud and Plowright in my *Tartuffe* translation at the Old Vic, and I wish I'd been in London to see it. (I did see a review of that production, in which the critic cited my rhyming of 'fossil' and 'docile', and said 'Mr Wilbur is evidently an American.') I've heard good things about a number of subsequent productions, among them, a *Misanthrope* at the RSC and a recent smashing performance of *School for Wives* at the Almeida. It does seem that some English actors can handle a couplet handsomely, and a surprising number of North American actors have proven able to do so. In this regard, it's very good luck for our continent that Brian Bedford is on it; he superbly directed my translation of *Phèdre* at Stratford, Ontario, and there and on Broadway he has repeatedly shown the world, and other actors, how Molière in verse ought to be played.

There are, to be sure, actors who can't deal expressively with the rhythms of verse, and who don't know how to acknowledge the rhyme in a hit-and-run fashion. One otherwise charming Célimène said to me, after a Chicago performance of the *Misanthrope*, 'I can do anything by Tennessee Williams, but this new stuff is too much for me.' That so many actors find Molière's couplets actable is due in part to the fact that they do not forever click shut and stop the voice. Regardless of grammar and punctuation, the lines have a continual dramatic impetus and colloquial flow.

And they are helped in no small part here by the quality of the translations you have offered them.

Translating the living is very different from doing the safely dead. You, like many others, translated some of Brodsky's poems. Since he was also given to 'translating' his own work, I wonder, did he put his oar in, or leave you to get on with it?

The late Andrei Sergeiev told me, during or soon after my first visit to Russia, that the very best translations of my work had been done by Joseph Brodsky, and that they couldn't be published because Brodsky was in disfavour with the authorities. When Brodsky left Russia and came to the States, his friend Carl Proffer invited me to translate 'The Funeral of Bobò', and I worked very hard on it for a number of weeks – wanting to get it just right because Joseph was reputed to be fussy, and because he had reportedly done so well by me. I recall that, sending the translation to Proffer, I asked Joseph's permission to toss the phrase 'pregnant with his message' into the penultimate line, and that I was allowed to do so. In the case of 'Six Years Later', there was a little putting-in of the oar by Joseph. Some time after the appearance of my version in the *New Yorker*, Joseph came out to my house in Cummington to tell me that he and Derek Walcott, during a return flight from some poetry function in Oklahoma, had brooded over the last stanza and made some revisions in it. I didn't think the changes an improvement, but told Joseph by all means to incorporate them in his upcoming book. As for my then upcoming book, my *New and Collected*, it contains the unimproved version of the translation. Joseph thought for a time, quite wrongly, that I was touchy about the matter, but we remained good friends. I always prized his perfectionism, though it made him harshly downright at times; a little scorn can be a precious thing in a slack age. His translations of seven of my poems, by the way, were published after the advent of Yeltsin in *Novy Mir*.

You have written one or two 'dialogue' poems but your main dramatic interest is revealed in your translations of plays. Drama, not to say comedy, in heroic couplets, as we've discussed, is a tall order in English, but you seem to have enjoyed and risen to the challenge. Do you find formal tight-spots like that inspiring? Samuel Daniel wrote of rhyme forcing a poet to heights he would otherwise have missed or failed to rise up to. It is an idea you have frequently spoken of in your own defence of formal ways of writing.

If an artist has patience and ability, I think that he'll always benefit from some resistance in the medium, and that resistance will be converted to a greater power in the work. The resistance of heroic couplets is superable, and the 'formal tight-spots' one gets in and out of in translating Molière are indeed inspiring. By slowing you down, and putting you under inventive pressure, they make for a fidelity that is also fresh. I think that Samuel Daniel was right.

I have side-tracked myself. I meant to reflect on the fact that you have successfully completed large works of translation in drama while confining your own work mainly to the lyric. Looking at History and the Dream Songs *as sequences, as mentioned earlier, you may feel quite justified in avoiding the large-scale, but dramatic form does seem to be another alternative for a large poem. Were there any other factors, such as the slots or windows of time that were available in your teaching schedules, that kept you from trying a dramatic alternative?*

When I tried a verse play in 1952, sitting in an adobe house in New Mexico, it turned out that I wasn't any good at breaking myself down into a cast of characters. That discovery led directly to my translating *The Misanthrope* as an alternative from which I might incidentally learn something about poetry on stage. That play was such a pleasure to do, and had such success when performed in Cambridge and New York, that I adjusted my theatrical ambitions accordingly and went on to do playable versions of a number of classical French plays. In 1955, the theatre enlisted me in another way, when Lillian Hellman and Lenny Bernstein invited me to do (and in some cases re-do) the lyrics for their musical-in-progress, *Candide*. The show had some inherent difficulties (such as the fact that the plot, like Voltaire's, told the same joke over and over), and no production has ever been wholly satisfactory. But owing to the vitality of the music, *Candide* has been continually revived and revised, and I've repeatedly written fresh material, most recently for the National Theatre's well-received production of 1999. In the middle 1960s I wrote the lyrics for a musical version of Giraudoux's *Madwoman of Chaillot*, and when that project blew up at the casting phase because our producer had lost control of the adaptation rights, I decided that musical Show Biz was too wasteful of effort, and took my leave of it. Whether I shall ever go back to my abandoned verse play, I can't say; I think I may be diversified enough as it is.

While we are on the topic of longer, more dramatic works, I find it interesting that in the piece he wrote for the Partisan Review *back in 1990, J. D. McClatchy wrote of you: 'Yet Wilbur's theme is precisely this Stevensian "nothing that is", insinuating itself into our thoughts, our souls, ever since "the garden where we first mislaid / Simplicity of wish and will". "Lying" joins a trio of other poems from earlier collections – "In Limbo", "The Mind-Reader", and "Walking to Sleep" – that brood on in-between states, the borders of consciousness. They are looser, longer than Wilbur's other poems, tentative explorations ... and they show to best advantage his dramatic abilities and mastery of psychological nuance that in other, more formally rigorous poems are concentrated in a single image.' And he wishes there were more like them. So I am going to ask why there weren't more poems like them in your work? They have been highly rated by a number of commentators.*

I agree with Sandy McClatchy that the poems he names are among my best, and I hope to write more of that brooding kind, which so often find themselves exploring the marchlands of consciousness. It's in the nature of such poems that they gather in and constellate many thoughts and images which have been randomly waiting in the mind, sometimes for a good while. For me, at any rate, such marshallings and moppings-up can happen only so often.

The range of your work is probably not remarked so clearly over here as it should be. Does the attention given to some of your work, and the neglect of other parts, on either side of the Atlantic, surprise or disappoint you?

My daughter Ellen is putting together her second book of short fiction; my son Christopher, a senior software designer, is a great reader and linguist; my son Nathan is a textbook editor and licensed landscape architect; my son Aaron, who had the bad luck to be born autistic, is nonetheless happy and musical and holds down a job in the world. These lively people were lively children, well worth playing with, and reading to, and making up bedtime stories for. Thanks to them, I have a lasting purchase on the child's sense of things. Children, I think, are anxious for order, but are not yet taken in by adult categories and pretences. My children's books, *Opposites* and *More Opposites* (for which I also did the illustrations), are full of little poems which subvert conventional patterns of thinking, and a more recent book, *The Disappearing Alphabet*, undermines reality in its own way. So long as it's amusing, children relish a bit of unease.

I'd rather like to see some critic connect those playful books with the rest of me – though I can't complain, on the whole, of my treatment by anthologists and commentators. Were I to complain of anything, it would be of the fact that not all of my work is available in other English-speaking countries. It's a publisher's maxim that 'plays don't sell', and no doubt there's some truth in the saying. Still, it vexes me that my Molière translations can be seen on the stage in the U.K. or South Africa or Australia, but not readily found in a bookstore there. I wish too that my books of prose pieces – *Responses* and *The Catbird's Song* – were more available abroad, if only for the Poe essays that are in them.

In your Shenandoah *piece, which I mentioned earlier, you remark that question-times at public readings could be a strain on your 'good citizenship' in the frequent requirement for explication that you felt would only dilute and falsify the poem in question. You also felt that the desire for background and information was often stronger than the wish for any direct experience of actual poems. Some of this may have been a concomitant of the readings so common in university and educational establishments, but how do you cope with this sort of thing now? At the risk of asking you to enter a Chinese box, I include things like this interview.*

Bill Williams once quoted somebody as remarking that if there were two doors, one labelled 'This way to see God' and the other labelled 'This way to a lecture about God', most people would flock to the second door. There are indeed people who want to know not poetry but the poetry situation. And there are critics who give such folk what, for some reason, they want – assigning all the poets to schools and tendencies, and writing sentences like 'The Beat poets rose up against the conformity of the Eisenhower era'. I'm not good at being quizzed about the Big Picture. There are also abrasive persons whose questions one doesn't want to answer – people like the angry girl who confronted me after a reading at Amherst, demanding 'Do you read any but Establishment poets? Do you read Latino poets? Black poets? Gay and Lesbian poets? Native American poets?' I told her that I liked a good poem by anybody, but that a poor poem was not enhanced by its sexual slant or ethnic origin. She shook her head vigorously throughout my reply.

Mostly, however, I can handle whatever I'm asked – having been at it for some decades – and am glad to do so. I'm gratified when people take the trouble to come out and hear me, or write and say that some lines of mine have mattered to them, and I think I owe their enquiries a civil response. After all, I too have questions to ask about poems which engage me, and the poets who wrote them: I wish I could interrogate Milton about that two-handed engine in 'Lycidas'.

All interviews, however pleasant and animated, have one disturbing aspect. The interview form would seem to absolve the interviewee of egotism – after all, he is being repeatedly prompted to speak of himself; yet as he hears himself say 'I' for the two hundredth time, he strikes himself as appallingly self-important, and wishes he could reply in Japanese, which is rumoured to have no first person pronoun. (Can that be true?)

But another problem, I think, arises in public readings – which might, indeed, encourage a form of repetition. Emily Dickinson said that the pen has many inflections but the voice only one – at a time, she means. This is perhaps more a readings problem with your earlier work with its use of ambivalence and reanimation of derivations and roots. How do you cope with this limitation of the voice?

Back in the 1950s, after I'd given a reading at NYU, a woman rose in the audience and said 'Young man, why do you sound like a minister?' I don't know what denomination she had in mind, but I believe I know what she meant. She was referring to my hectoring desire to imprint the full sense of my words on the hearer's mind. I now know that that generally can't be done, and have modulated toward the dramatic, but I still convey as much as I can of what's on the page. I read clearly, so that the words can be grasped as well as heard; I don't act the lines, but gesture with the voice toward the sounds I'd make if I were acting.

That sounds quite difficult to do.

If a poem is comparatively simple, or if I'm reading from one of my translated plays I get a little more Thespian. There are some poems whose chief subtlety is a matter of tone, and it's such poems, above all, which have not been fully published until they have been read aloud.

Back to writing. Your skill with movement and actions, with verbs in strong rhymed positions, has been well commented upon by Hecht and others. He speaks of it as natural, instinctive quality in your work, but is it really so, or was it something you had to work at, acquire?

When you ask me that, I recollect how as a child I liked to draw pictures of football action, or of baseball players diving for catches or sliding into bases. Though my draftsmanship is still imperfect, I find that, when I do cartoons for children's books, the thing I most surely capture is bodily motion. I seem to take a natural delight in evoking physical movement, whether in pictures or in poems – and in the poems, that taste consorts very well with my liking for concreteness. I feel, in fact, that whether or not one is conveying specific objective motions, the body and all its movements and timings are a vital part of any poetry. Yeats's narcotic early talk about 'spiritual and unemphatic rhythms' never sounded appealing or spiritual to me.

George Seferis wrote something similar in his diary: 'In essence, the poet has one theme: his live body.'
 What was sometimes unsettling in your early work was a sense that you wrote a sort of lexicon language, a vocabulary of words from any period and style of English to accommodate formal structures.

If by 'accommodating formal structures' you mean that I'd be capable of digging up a dead word like 'yclept' in order to rhyme with 'slept', I plead innocent.

No, nothing as extreme as that. I'm talking about the same thing McClatchy speaks of in the piece I mentioned a moment ago. Some of the early poems, he says, 'are written in a rather stagey dialect of their own, one that prefers "fane" to "grove" or "espial" to "sight."' Was this just part of a learning curve, or a deliberate distancing effect?

I think that I've never chosen any words for formal reasons only, or out of a wish to be quaint and curious. But I concede to you and McClatchy that there's some 'lexicon language' in my poems, especially in the earlier books. I've enjoyed pointedly reviving the root meanings of words like 'ramify' and 'superb', and as a reader I've enjoyed the same sort of serious wordplay in Stevens and Ransom. If I can do it without mystification, I like to call a raceme a raceme. And once or twice I've made up a word like 'revenance' in 'In the Elegy Season', because our lexicon seemed to need it for the expression of an idea.

Yes. It's basically a matter of fine judgement whether the poem enlivens a word or root meaning, or whether the word deadens the poem.

Sandy McClatchy is right about this matter, as he tends to be about matters generally, but I take exception to the two examples he gives. In 'Children of Darkness', of which we were speaking earlier, the opening question might be paraphrased this way: 'If forest trees and glades are like sacred architecture, as the old poets say, why are these woods full of evil-looking fungi?' The first line – 'If groves are choirs and sanctuaried fanes' – might echo or suggest Shakespeare's 'bare ruined choirs', a woodland passage of 'Il Penseroso', and William Cullen Bryant's 'The groves were God's first temples'. I think that 'fanes', an old-fashioned poetic word meaning 'temples', is pretty much to my purpose in that line, and I hope the purpose gets across. In any case, I was not trying to be charmingly obsolete.

Though some might think that, apart from the rhyme requirement, 'shrines', say, might have been adequate enough and without problem.

I would also defend my use of 'espials' (in 'The Eye'), on grounds of accuracy. If you are toying with a pair of binoculars, as happens in that poem, and find yourself tempted to be a voyeur, you are surely hoping for furtive 'espials' rather than mere 'sights'.

Or peeping, as in Tom. Though I've used both of your choices of word myself in period translations. And it may amuse you to know that 'Revenance' has been a recent UK book title, a novel, I seem to remember.
  But to more mundane matters. May I ask the usual questions about your work methods – whether you use a typewriter, word-processor, pen and paper, tape-recorder?

I have no computer, fax machine, copier, electric pencil-sharpener, or other technology – though I have at times used a tape-player when composing show-lyrics.

Do you work in silence or like background sound?

As a young man I could write in a troop-train, a park, a hotel lobby, a living-room full of children – anywhere, in fact, with the exception of a

Paris café. Now that I am less insulated and spellbound by work in progress, I do best in a quiet study or bookish outbuilding, where my wife Charlee can let me know by buzzer if the telephone is unavoidably for me.

Is there anyone whose judgement of drafts you like to rely on? Someone said you were willing to hear advice but it seldom changed your decisions in composition.

Charlee has always been the first and most trusted reader of my poems, and as one who played in Molière scenes and Musset curtain-raisers at school, she passes expertly on every line of my translations from French drama. In my earlier days at Harvard, I used to trade poems once a month with Richard Eberhart, John Ciardi, John Holmes and May Sarton. Once, during that time, Robert Frost said to me, 'I hear you've been meeting with some other poets. What are you looking for, criticism?' 'No,' I said, 'praise.' 'Oh,' he said, 'that's all right, then.' I've shown my poems since to a number of honest and magnanimous friends, among them John Brinnin, Bill Meredith, Tony Hecht, Jimmy Merrill. Bill and Sonja Smith have been patient readers of my translations from the French, and Bill has more than once ordered the contents of a book of poems for me – a thing I have no notion of how to do. In the case of my translations, I've often made changes on the advice of such counsellors as Merrill and McClatchy. Jimmy saved me from gawkiness in the rendering of a Dante tercet, and from bathos in rendering a line of Racine, and rewrote, in fact, a couplet of my *Phèdre* translation. When it comes to my poems, if my wife and friends are unenthusiastic I am less likely to improve a poem than to discard it or set it aside. When Cal Lowell disliked a poem of mine called 'Leaving', I suppressed it for a decade, but then got pigheaded and published it.

No poet these days ever escapes with just being a poet. You taught and you also worked as a general editor of the Laurel Series of Poets with the Dell Publishing Company. Did you find this a drag or a stimulation for your own work? How time-consuming was it? Did you commission much or even discover any interesting poems or poets?

It took a great deal of hard work to general-edit that paperback series of classic English and American poets, and inevitably it took me away from writing poems. But it was worth it. Extraordinarily fine people agreed to edit the volumes: Dudley Fitts, Howard Nemerov, John Wain, Reuben Brower, W. H. Auden, and many others. We had classy introductions, well-chosen texts, good notes and other apparatus. For a few years there you could, trotting through any air terminal in America, pick up for 35c a handsomely designed book of Marvell, or Whittier, or Browning, Herbert, Dickinson, Spenser, Whitman, Pope ... the whole crew.

While talking editorially, I wonder what your interest in Witter Bynner was? He is not at all well known over here.

When I was invited, in the mid-'70s, to choose and introduce a *Selected Poems* of Witter Bynner, I did so partly to oblige my friend and Wesleyan colleague Paul Horgan, who'd known Bynner well in Santa Fe and who wanted me to do the job. I was also attracted to the assignment by my mistrust of parroting academics who know for certain what is 'major', and my curiosity about a poet who had once been esteemed and was now forgotten. At the time, I knew nothing of Bynner's but *The Jade Mountain*, his spare and able translations from the Chinese. Bynner turned out not to be major, but I found him a versatile and interesting poet whose best work – the volume *Indian Earth*, for example – deserved to be back in print. His early models, by the way, were Whitman on the one hand and on the other Housman, with whom he corresponded and from whom he received criticism and encouragement.

Yes, he has some curious overlaps and near overlaps of phrasing with Housman which seem coincidences more than anything else. And later he went a bit Lawrentian.
You were American Poet Laureate during 1987-88. How different is the job from the British one? (Quite a few British poets regard the native 'post' as the kiss of death when they look back on the previous 'illustrious' holders of the position, and regard Larkin's hesitation or unwillingness to do it as a mark of his genuineness.) The American system is clearly very different, and not life-long – since Ted Hughes's death nor is ours – but what are you supposed to do or achieve in your spell? Fifty-odd laureates a century seems a daunting number, from over here.

For many decades, a procession of poets – among them Aiken, Frost, Jarrell, Bishop – held a position entitled Consultant in Poetry to the Library of Congress. When, in the middle 1980s, the poetry-loving Senator Spark Matsunaga at last persuaded Congress that the nation should honour poetry by creating a laureateship, a new title was tacked onto the old consultancy and Robert Penn Warren became our first poet laureate. Because his health was failing, Warren had to limit his activities in that role, and it was I, as his successor, who first learned what the new title would entail. Whereas 'consultant' had been, to say the least, an unexciting job-description in Washington, the glossy words 'poet laureate' alerted all the media, and I found myself doing numberless interviews in which the first question was always, 'What does the Poet Laureate do?' The answer was that he gives interviews; that he advises the library in its poetry-recording and lecture programmes, and introduces the lecturers; that he delivers at the Library an annual reading and lecture of his own; that he answers a lot of mail, receives schoolchildren and other visitors in his office, makes a few ceremonial appearances, and often reads his poems in the capital and elsewhere. Though the job had its satisfactions, I found it at once too little and too much: it didn't accomplish quite enough, or sufficiently use my best abilities; and because I am not very well organized, my commutings to Washington and my duties there disrupted my real work.

Later Laureates, I gather, have been encouraged by the Library to exploit the exposure which the new title brings, and to seek in one way or another to bring poetry to a larger public. Our American laureates are not expected to produce timely poems on matters of national concern. Red Warren announced, at the time of his appointment, that he didn't intend to write 'get-well-quick poems for Reagan's sick horse'. The position, though scarcely comparable to the English original, is perhaps more honourable, because its holders, and the consultants who preceded them, have thus far been of consistently good quality.

Perhaps the laureateship should not be a job at all, but simply an honour. In any event, what matters most to me about this recent institution is that my country has wished to show respect for the art of poetry.

Certainly the post is not likely to bring the poet into disrepute as the English one seems to do – in time at least, and among the cognoscenti. God knows how Ted Hughes could accept the job.

But speaking of jobs in libraries, are you a hoarder of papers and files or a shredder? How 'complete' will your archive be? Will it all go to the same location?

All of my drafts and proofs and notebooks and sketches and other papers, including whatever incoming mail is of interest, go to the Amherst library. What I don't do is to make and save copies of the letters I write to others; that would take the spontaneity and one-to-one genuineness out of letter-writing.

Have many of your works, besides 'On Freedom's Ground', been set to music?

My show-lyrics have been set by Bernstein, of course, and also by Michel Legrand. A number of my poems have been set by such composers as Yehudi Wyner, Randall Thompson, John Corigliano, Ron Perera, and Arnold Black. I know that I'm forgetting some important names, but there's a sampling. Arnie Black's settings are unusual in that they allow the poems to be intelligibly spoken in and through the music. (A good many settings of poems, nowadays, could only be described as sensitive but obliterative responses.)

Richard Winslow asked me, in the late '50s, to write a seasonal hymn for an upcoming Smith-Wesleyan Christmas concert, and set the resultant text very inventively for tenor, harpsichord, and oboe. In more orthodox settings, the hymn now appears in a number of church hymnals, despite the fact that one of its lines ('For stony hearts of men') has troubled some hymnal-committees because of its 'exclusive language'. A Roman Catholic hymnbook high-handedly altered the line to read 'For hearts made hard by sin', and the Anglican Church of Canada, when I couldn't accept their proposed revision of the line, rather pettishly broke off negotiations. If I really thought that a sensible woman would feel excluded by my use of the word 'men', I'd hasten to change the line myself. The hymn, by the way, is a challenging form in which to compose, because one is not entitled to be quirky, but must say what some hundreds of faithful people will be able to stand and belt out in good conscience.

Poetry has obviously cost a number of your contemporaries a good deal, but not all of the difficulties of being a poet are so dramatically apparent. Looking back on your career, if you could have foreseen it, would you have chosen any other one in preference? Or would you say a real poet is never given that option?

I was a competent teacher, and might have been competent in journalism, and a few other professions. But in poetry I had a gift, and if you have a gift (as opposed to a competence) there's an obligation to exercise it. Furthermore, it's a joy to have some ability in which you can surprise yourself, and unaccountably rise above your own level. To devote yourself to a gift can mean moonlighting, fatigue, self-doubt, financial uncertainty, and other trials. If I have gotten away with being a poet, it has had a great deal to do with my marriage in 1942 to a woman whom Willa Muir called 'a perfect poet's wife' – a partner, muse, and friend who is even surer than I that poems are necessary.

I think we'd better say 'a poet's perfect wife'.

I think I quote Willa correctly, but I see your point; let's compromise by saying 'a perfect wife for a poet'.

You said earlier that you sometimes had help from a friend in arranging a book. Did you have help with your latest book, Mayflies?

Yes, Bill Smith looked over the manuscript, threw out a poem or so, and divided the text into two parts, giving the second part the title of 'Transformations'. He's an extremely good shaper of books. I'm not. The best I can do by way of arrangement is to follow a long poem by a short, or relieve one mood by another.

Are all the poems in Mayflies *new, or have some been maturing since before your* New and Collected? *I ask because you've said that it can take you a long time to generate a poem.*

Except for the two Baudelaire translations, the book is all new work; it was all done – and slowly done, as always – since my last *New and Collected* of 1988. The Baudelaires were first translated, at the request of Marthiel and Jackson Matthews, for their 1955 New Directions edition of *The Flowers of Evil*. I've slightly tinkered with the translations since, and when I was assembling *Mayflies* it seemed about time to include them in one of my collections. Baudelaire's albatross-poet is insufferably self-pitying and self-admiring, yet the poem is a beauty and I hope to have captured some of it.

So you have retained the mix of original verse and translations that's been a feature of your earlier collections.
  I can see why you would have a go at Baudelaire's 'Albatross' and Mallarmé's 'Sea Breeze', but Canto xxv of the Inferno *again surprises a bit, given all that you might have chosen. Was it your fascination with movement – the canto is crammed with shifts and changes – that drew you to it? It's not a canto most people turn to in Dante – certainly not those who do a one-off.*

When Dan Halpern of Ecco Press was arranging for the *Inferno* to be translated by various hands, I eagerly chose Canto xxv from among those not yet spoken for by Seamus Heaney, Bill Merwin, and other worthies. Certainly I was drawn to it by what Jimmy Merrill, in his introduction to the Ecco volume, called 'the proto-Baroque effect' of its 'double metamorphosis' – all that intricate and astonishing change and movement. I also wanted to confront the canto's peculiar challenge, and see if I could not, while preserving the terza rima form, convey Dante at his most complex in the spare, plain Dantean manner. And there were other attractions as well: I wanted to do right by the great similes of burning paper and darting hedge-lizards, and by the elegant lines which recollect the metamorphoses in Lucan and Ovid.

Douglas R. Hofstadter was very impressed with your version of Dante and regretted that you had not done more. We've touched before on the workload of a major translation. It took Binyon seventeen years, I believe, to do the Commedia. *Were you frightened of getting hooked on it?*

Various people – among them James Merrill and John Frederick Nims – thought well enough of my canto to raise the possibility of my doing Dante, or his infernal portion at any rate, in toto. Two things have deterred me. It took me a very long time to do Canto xxv, and preserving the form of the original (which seemed to me obligatory) involved such fascinating difficulties that I often felt I was on a suicide mission. At the age of seventy-nine, I am not sure that I have the time to win thirty-three more battles of the kind, let alone ninety-nine. And so for the present I am hanging back, and waiting perhaps for an access of folly.

Another reason is this: there are a number of highly accomplished renderings of Dante – I think of Longfellow, Ciardi, and Mandelbaum, to speak of American translators only.

There's Pinsky's Inferno *too, which is odd but interesting, with some half-rhymes, and rearrangements of line order.*

Even if I had the good fortune to improve on them, I couldn't make such a difference as I've made by fifty years' work on Molière. When I commenced work on Molière, he was seldom read, taught, or performed in our country – save, of course, in French. There were no fully faithful versions of the great verse plays, and prose translations of his œuvre were mostly quite leaden. I'm glad to have done something about that situation. It seems to me that one consideration for the translator, apart from his own pleasure and special abilities, should be the needs and lacks of the culture. If I do any more big translations, I feel at present that they should be of Molière, whom I've learned to do properly, or of his French contemporaries; maybe I should have a go at Racine's only comedy, *Les Plaideurs.*

In our earlier technical discussions we didn't touch on syllabics. I must say I received a real shock in reading part 2 of 'A Wall in the Woods: Cummington'. One verse that drew my attention looked like involving, literally, a desperate measure for a poet like Wilbur:

> There is no tracing
> The leaps and scurries with which
> He braids his long castle, ra-
> Cing, by gap, ledge, niche ...

I'm referring to the last two lines, of course. I first thought you were trying to hide the rhyme 'tracing/racing' to account for the odd split of word. Then I realized you were combining a syllable count with rhyme and metre of a type. The rhyme is full, more or less, in verse two and the last. And, of course, despite the disguise, here. But the split still seems rather unfortunate.

You've caught me in what may be an outrageous experiment. When 'A Wall in the Woods' was reprinted in *The Best American Poetry 1990*, I contributed – as the poets were asked to do – a little note on the poem. It read, 'This poem is in two voices, the second opposing whatever there is of elegiac sadness in the first. I suppose that 'A Wall in the Woods' may raise the question of whether a two-part poem can effectively shift from blank verse to syllabics. But perhaps not: the rhythms of part 2 are apparently strong enough to have disguised, for some good readers, the 5775 syllable pattern which I used in hopes of embodying the fluent skittering of the chipmunk. Yes, it is a chipmunk. Two of my correspondents, neither a New Englander, took it to be a bird; but it seems to me that I give sufficient evidence for its being Tamias striatus...'

I wanted, then, to avoid metrical regularity in part 2, so as to embody something of the 'fluent skittering' of a chipmunk who weaves his way through and along a rough stone old wall, unpredictably appearing and disappearing. Further to emphasize that unpredictability, I decided that, in the third line of each stanza, the rhyme should vary in placement and strength: thus in the first stanza 'guff' rhymes with a non-terminal 'duff', and in the fourth stanza the first syllable of 'Cyclopean' rhymes with the third syllable of 'Sentry-like'. The rhyme of 'tracing' with 'ra-/cing', which you note and find disturbing, is part of the same high-jinks: in splitting the latter word, I felt as if I were seeing a chipmunk vanish around a rock.

Ah, shades of the 'spilling' stanzas of 'A Baroque Wall-Fountain in Vialla Sciarra. I'm sorry, I'm more conscious of the broken word than I am of the vanishing chipmunk.

As I offer that explanation, I feel as if one of the New Critics of my youth were frowning at me and speaking of the Fallacy of Imitative Form. One of my friends and advisors – I think it may have been Bill Smith – thought that the inconsistent rhyme was an aesthetic mistake; Merrill and Brinnin, on the other hand, felt that it worked pretty well.

I'd like to stay with the poem for a moment: like so many poets writing syllabics in English, you've chosen here lines of uneven syllables, 5, 7, 7, 5. The usual reason given is for poets to escape the even syllable numbers of iambics and trochaics but, knowing your experience of French, one is tempted to think you were having a sort of personal game with the alexandrine. Were you?

I see what you mean, and certainly my mind is haunted by the undulations of the alexandrine. But I don't think that I was playing any conscious game with that measure. My guess is that the 5 and 7 syllables came to me from my familiarity with the haiku form.

Have you done any pure and simple syllabics, any with even counts?

Well, there are those three poems I mentioned earlier, in which the haiku is used as a stanza. In *The Mind-Reader*, I published a haiku called 'Sleepless at Crown Point', and my new book has a group of three tankas in it. 'Wyeth's Milk Cans', in *New and Collected*, consists of two stanzas of 6, 7, and 5 syllables each, though it could readily be understood as trimeter throughout.

Yes, a plurality of stanzas may be the secret. After all, if you've a one-stanza poem, it might be considered rough metrics, stress verse or free verse, if you ever feel the need to enquire into its rhythmic structure. The repeats are needed to establish pattern. You make clear in two stanzas, in the Wall poem we've just looked at, the pattern you are going to make variations on.

My guess is that most experienced readers of English verse can hear syllabic quantity with some precision, so long as the lines are very short. But once the lines get beyond seven syllables or so, syllable-count can no longer be heard, and is useful only to the poet, as an arbitrary discipline.

Yes, and the count, it seems to me, has to be odd. We are so used to the species of metric known by some as accentual-syllabic.
You made me wary with your split rhyme. I checked part 1 of the poem: the eleven syllabled lines come randomly as with good blank verse. Auden frequently combined a pretty strict use of mixed metres and odd syllable count, some of which could be seen as splitting a pentameter. Were you attracted by his techniques?

Long ago, when I was writing a review of Auden's book *Nones*, I recall counting the syllables of his superb poem 'In Praise of Limestone', and discovering that the lines were alternatively 11 and 14. But in general, while enjoying Auden's formal power, I haven't found myself analyzing him technically. Why? I think it's because his really good poems are all of a piece: the elements of performance and technical play are so fused with the mood and tone and developing thought that I don't think of separating the form from the rest and crying 'What deftness!' or 'What rigour!' He's not, in my experience, the sort of writer whose art reduces readily to craft. Yet of course I've always been aware of his virtuosity, and his mixing of modes in sectioned poems, and I'm sure that I've learned from him in an osmotic way, without being brainy about it.

Your title poem 'Mayflies' reminded me of a passage in Laforgue, verse seven of 'Complainte des Mounis du Mont-Martre' :

> Moucherons, valseurs d'un soir de soleil,
> Vous, tout comme nous, nerfs de la nature,
>   Vous n'avez point cure
> De ce que peut être cette aventure:
> Les mondes penseurs s'errant au Soleil!

Do you know the poem?

People are forever making anthologies of cat-poems and dog-poems, but I don't think there are any anthologies of insect-poems, as there well might be. For as soon as you think of the possibility, there's a rustic somewhere in Spenser who brushes away a swarm of gnats and 'mars their murmurings', and there's Blake's fly, and the fly and bee of Dickinson, and the louse of Burns, the grasshopper and ant of La Fontaine, the white-tailed hornet and 'considerable speck' of Frost, the ladybird of Mother Goose ...

Keats wrote about gnats, of course, and there are midges doing things in Hecht ...

There are all sorts of poems which take insects (and bugs) lightly or seriously, and I think that such poems are often more individual, less predictable in their perspectives, than are poems about the other creatures. A friend of mine wrote me, regarding 'Mayflies', that it 'describes what we trout fishpersons know as "the evening hatch".' Though not at all insensitive to what my poem was saying, he couldn't help investing it with a sportsman's thoughts about fly-tying and the hope of trout. The lines which you quote from Laforgue, and which I've not encountered before, feel very akin to mine: his midges are dancers in the light of evening, and energies of nature like ourselves. I shall look up the poem when I get back to my library in Cummington. Is 'mounis' a misprint for 'minous'?

Goodness, I hope not. No, 'mounis' are ascetics, Hindu monks of some sort.

It has often been said that married love is difficult to be poetic about, yet you manage it in 'For C', a poem that is clearly the product of long experience, and the sort of thing you'd have to introduce at a reading by saying, 'It will take you forty years to understand this poem – and a marriage.' As you get older, one may wonder about one's youthful enthusiasms. On the other hand, there are poems that youth doesn't appreciate. May I close by asking if there are poems that you've come to appreciate in recent years which you didn't appreciate earlier just because you hadn't lived long enough? Chunks of Four Quartets *that I never used to rate now impinge, so that Eliot is having the last laugh, even if it's 'only the laceration of laughter that ceases to amuse'.*

I've always felt that when I grew up, I would grow attuned to the relative austerity of *Paradise Regained*, but that hasn't happened. May I live a little longer, and do it justice. There's a poem of Frost's – 'To Earthward' – which young readers don't grasp very easily, because it has to do with eros and ageing; but I have come to understand it very well. And then there's mortality and mutability. For much of my life I have expressed gracious and often sincere regret at the deaths of others, without much sense that my own was impending. Now I respond more deeply to the music of completion in Keats's 'To Autumn', and I think often of a phrase of Chesterton's – 'the decent inn of death'. Having seen much change, especially of late, I am more touched than formerly by Hardy's poem about the garden bench.

When E.B. White was asked by the *Times* how it felt to be 80, he replied that he couldn't say, because he was still inwardly 18. To some extent that's true of me too; at any rate, I enjoy a double purchase on things. Something in me keeps exclaiming, 'O brave new world,' and something else replies, 'Tis new to thee.'

≡

Mayflies

In sombre forest, when the sun was low,
I saw from unseen pools a mist of flies
    In their quadrillions rise
And animate a ragged patch of glow
With sudden glittering – as when a crowd
    Of stars appear
Through a brief gap in black and driven cloud,
One arc of their great round-dance showing clear.

It was no muddled swarm I witnessed, for
In *entrechats* each fluttering insect there
    Rose two steep yards in air,
Then slowly floated down to climb once more,
So that they all composed a manifold
    And figured scene,
And seemed the weavers of some cloth of gold,
Or the fine pistons of some bright machine.

Watching those lifelong dancers of a day
As night closed in, I felt myself alone
    In a life too much my own,
More mortal in my separateness than they –
Unless, I thought, I had been called to be
    Not fly or star
But one whose task is joyfully to see
How fair the fiats of the caller are.

Richard Wilbur

BIBLIOGRAPHY

Compiled by John Lancaster and Jack W. C. Hagstrom

It is in the nature of bibliographical listings that the compilers can never be absolutely certain that they know of all relevant publications, even when (as in our case) the author himself has provided assistance in finding them. We would be grateful, therefore, to hear from anyone who can identify omissions or errors, which will be corrected in our forthcoming full-scale descriptive bibliography that is the basis for this shorter listing. We have not included here RW's extensive juvenile writings; those and his writings while at Amherst College and during World War II are discussed in: John Lancaster and Jack W. C. Hagstrom, 'Richard Wilbur's Early Writing: Amherst College and World War II', in *War, Literature & the Arts*, v. 10, no. 1 (Spring/Summer, 1998), pp. 24-36.

The short-title listing below consists almost exclusively of writings by RW, rather than about him (a brief summary of secondary literature, with further references, appears at the end). RW's writings have been divided into eight major categories: POETRY, CANDIDE, TRANSLATIONS, PROSE, WORKS EDITED, WORKS FOR CHILDREN AND LIGHT VERSE, RECORDINGS, AND INTERVIEWS. A separate headnote to each section discusses characteristics peculiar to it.

Within some of the categories, works are further subdivided. MAJOR BOOK PUBLICATIONS are works that were overseen by RW and distributed through mainstream trade channels. LIMITED EDITION [ETC.] PUBLICATIONS comprises all manner of separately-printed items, ranging from Christmas cards printing a single poem, to elaborate illustrated broadsides, to programmes and menus for special events. What they have in common is that they are not mainstream publications, and they are separate printings (not part of a larger work). The UNCOLLECTED sub-category records poems, translations, prose, and works for children that have not appeared in any of the books listed in MAJOR BOOK PUBLICATIONS.

– JL, JWCH

PRIMARY WORKS

POETRY

MAJOR BOOK PUBLICATIONS

The Beautiful Changes, Reynal and Hitchcock, New York, 1947.
Ceremony, Harcourt, Brace and Co., New York, 1950.
Things of This World, Harcourt, Brace and Co., New York, 1956.
Poems 1943-1956 (a selection from the first three books), Faber and Faber, London, 1957.
Advice to a Prophet, Harcourt, Brace and World, New York, 1961/Faber and Faber, London, 1962.
Poems (reprints the first four collections), Harcourt, Brace and World, New York, 1963.
Walking to Sleep, Harcourt, Brace and World, New York, 1969/Faber and Faber, London, 1971.
The Mind-Reader, Harcourt Brace Jovanovich, New York, 1976/Faber and Faber, London, 1977.
New and Collected Poems (reprints the first six collections, omitting a few selections from play translations), Harcourt Brace Jovanovich, New York, 1988/Faber and Faber, London, 1989.
Mayflies, Harcourt, New York, San Diego, London, 2000.

LIMITED EDITION, PRIVATE PRESS, PERSONAL, BROADSIDE, AND SIMILAR PUBLICATIONS

'The Puritans', in *Two Poems and an Invitation*, an announcement of the Dartmouth College

Library Poetry Programme, May 5-6, 1949, in which RW and John Ciardi were the featured poets.

The Beautiful Changes, broadside, no. 5 in a series, Harvard University, Cambridge, Massachusetts, Poetry Room, 1947. Another edition printed as an announcement of RW's reading at Winthrop University, September 25, 1997.

A Black December Turkey, the Wilburs' Christmas card, 1953. Appears elsewhere as 'A Black November Turkey'.

Sonnet, the Wilburs' Christmas card, 1956.

Two Voices in a Meadow, the Wilburs' Christmas card, 1957. Later printed on the occasion of a reading by RW, November 15, 1985, New Traditions, Huntington, Massachusetts, 1985, 150 copies. Also separately printed as an insert to the programme for his reading at Dia, New York, May 14, 1991, 500 copies.

A Christmas Hymn, first separately printed for the Wesleyan University Candlelight Service, December 7, 1958. Also printed as the Wilburs' Christmas card, 1958. Later, in 1967, also printed for a service at Trinity Church, Portland, Connecticut, and again, in 1987, as a Christmas card for the Wilburs and two others.

Advice to a Prophet, 'American Arts Festival poem', broadside, DePauw University, Greencastle, Indiana, 1959, about 500 copies. Also printed as the Wilburs' Christmas card for 1959.

'Altitudes', included in the programme for the bicentennial celebration of the town of Amherst, Massachusetts, October 23-24, 1959.

Mind, broadside, reproduced from RW's manuscript fair copy, issued in a portfolio: *21 Etchings and Poems*, ed. by Peter Grippe, Morris Gallery, New York, 1960, 50 numbered copies and 12 artist's proofs. The poem was also printed as a broadside keepsake for a reading by RW at Smith College, April 1, 1978, 200 copies, 25 of which were distributed at a dinner the evening before, in a folder dated March 31.

Two Quatrains for First Frost, the Christmas card of Louise and Willard Lockwood, 1960.

The Proof, the Wilburs' Christmas card, 1963.

Seed Leaves, the Wilburs' Christmas card, 1964. Also included in RW's *Address Given at the Dedication of the Robert Frost Library, Amherst College*. Later separately published in book form, David R. Godine, Boston, Massachusetts, 1974, 160 copies.

On the Marginal Way, first printed as part of the menu and head-table guest list for the inaugural luncheon of Joseph C. Palamountain, Jr., as President of Skidmore College, September 25, 1965. Later published in book form by Adja Yunkers, New York, c. 1975, 25 copies.

Under Cygnus, the Wilburs' Christmas card, 1966.

A Wood, the Wilburs' Christmas card, 1967. Also printed as a broadside for a celebration of RW's appointment as Poet Laureate of the United States, March 7, 1988, 300 copies.

Complaint, The Phoenix Bookshop, New York, 1968, 100 numbered and 26 lettered copies.

A Late Aubade, the Wilburs' Christmas card, 1968. Also printed in a programme for RW's reading at SUNY-Brockport, March 12, 1969, about 200 copies.

A Wedding Toast, the Wilburs' Christmas card, 1971.

The Writer, broadside keepsake for members of the Grolier Club, from the Associates of the Godine Press, on the occasion of the opening of an exhibition of RW's work, May 13, 1972, 200 copies. Another broadside edition was printed for James Connolly in April, 1998, about 10 copies.

A Storm in April, the Wilburs' Christmas card, 1973. Also printed in *The Fourteenth Annual Wallace Stevens Program*, for which the presentation and a reading were by RW, April 6, 1977.

To His Skeleton, broadside, reproduced from RW's manuscript fair copy, International Poetry Forum, Carnegie Library, Pittsburgh, Pennsylvania, 1975, 500 copies. Distributed at a reading by RW and others, October 8, 1975.

Two Riddles from Aldhelm, broadside, Rook Press, Derry, Pennsylvania, 1975, in three issues of 100 copies each: signed, with an illustration; signed, without illustration; unsigned, without illustration.

A Black Birch in Winter, printed as a Christmas card for the Wilburs and for the publisher David Godine, 1975.

4/5/74, 'An Arts Action Press broadside', Hawthorne Press, Lenox, Massachusetts, 1976, 80 copies. Collected as 'April 5, 1974'.

In the Field, broadside, Sea Pen Press & Paper Mill, Seattle, Washington, 1978, 15 copies.

Alatus, broadside, issued in a portfolio: *For Robert Penn Warren, 24.IV.80*, 75 copies. Not originally issued separately, but separate copies are known.

Wyeth's Milk Cans, poster broadside, issued as part of the 'Poetry on the Buses' programme in Pittsburgh, Pennsylvania, July 10, 1980, 3,000 copies.

Seven Poems, Abattoir Editions, Omaha, Nebraska, 1981, 200 copies.

On Having Mis-identified a Wild Flower, poster broadside, issued as part of the 'Poetry on the Buses' programme in Pittsburgh, Pennsylvania, November 9, 1981, 1,000 copies.

Advice from the Muse, Deerfield Press, Deerfield, Massachusetts/Gallery Press, Dublin, 1981, 300 copies.

The Ride, broadside keepsake for a Grolier Club event, Jordan Davies, New York, 1982, 350 copies. Also reproduced from RW's fair copy in the programme of the International Poetry Forum's 20th anniversary celebration, October 19, 1986.

Hamlen Brook, a holiday greeting by the Wilburs and by the Albondocani Press and Ampersand Books, New York, 1982, 400 copies. Also printed in an announcement of a reading by RW at the Library of Congress, October 5, 1987, 2,000 copies. Also printed (together with James Merrill's 'Arabian Night') as a handout for 'An Evening with Two Great Poets', March 13, 1991, 250 copies.

Transit, broadside prepared by Jordan Davies in 1981 and intended for a Grolier Club exhibition, but never issued (proof copies exist). First printed as a broadside by The Folger Shakespeare Library, Washington, D.C., 1982, 200 copies. Another edition was privately printed as an invitation to a reading, April 19, 1983, 50 copies. A different edition was one of 22 broadsides included in a portfolio, 50 copies (some individual broadsides may have been privately available separately): *Fifty Years of American Poetry: A Tribute to Marie Bullock, 11 April 1984*, Palaemon Press, Winston-Salem, North Carolina, 1984. The poem was also printed in the programme for RW's appearance when giving the Marie Bullock Poetry Reading, Academy of American Poets, October 5, 1993. Included later in the New York Transit Authority's 'Poetry in Motion' series, 1995, 6,000 copies printed on one side, on card stock, 3,000 copies printed on both sides (one side in reverse), on translucent paper.

Two Poems, broadside, an insert in the programme for the 20th St. Botolph Club Foundation Award, presented to RW on December 8, 1983, 700 copies.

Teresa, broadside, one of a series, *The Printed Poem/The Poem as Print*, The Press at Colorado College, Colorado Springs, Colorado, 1985.

A Finished Man, Bits Press, Cleveland, Ohio, 1985, 50 copies.

Clearness, a New Year's card containing two stanzas, and sent by Amherst College to its alumni, January 1, 1986, 25,000 copies.

On Freedom's Ground: an American Cantata, set to music by William Schuman for the Statue of Liberty Centennial Gala, October 28, 1986, 2,600 copies distributed as a 4-page insert in the programme for the premiere performance, Avery Fisher Hall, Lincoln Center. Another edition was printed in a run of 4,000 copies, 2,000 for distribution at a dress rehearsal, and 2,000 for use at Crane School of Music performances later in the year.

Lying and Other Poems, Cummington Press, Omaha, Nebraska, 1987, 160 copies.

A Summer Morning, broadside, Library of Congress, Washington, D.C., 1988, 40 copies.

'Parable' and 'Exeunt', included in a programme insert for a concert by the University of Massachusetts Chamber Choir and Madrigal Singers, May 14, 1989, and accompanied by a musical setting of the poems by Robert Stern.

A Wall in the Woods: Cummington, keepsake for a conference that was cancelled, Sea Cliff Press, New York, distributed June 3, 1989, 150 copies. Also printed as a broadside for the 70th anniversary of the Cummington Community of the Arts, October 16, 1993, 100 copies.

Trolling for Blues, announcement of RW's tenure as Robert Frost Library Fellow, Amherst College, November 13-17, 1989, 2,500 copies.

A Barred Owl, broadside, printed for an RW evening at the Grolier Club, New York, Sea Cliff Press, 1992, about 100 copies. Other editions: broadside, Turret Bookshop, London, 1992, 200 copies; announcing a reading by RW, April 29, 1993, in the Distinguished American Poets Series at County College of Morris Randolph, New Jersey; broadside, on the occasion of a poetry reading at South Congregational Church, Amherst, Massachusetts, 150 copies.

A Digression, broadside, Aralia Press, West Chester, Pennsylvania, 1995, 150 copies.

Three Poems, Dugdemona Press, Tuscaloosa, Alabama, 1995, 65 copies.

Italy: Maine, broadside, issued for participants in a session on RW's war poetry at the American Literature Association's annual conference, May 24, 1997, 125 copies. Restores the original text of the first line, which had been editorially altered for the poem's first appearance, in the *Saturday Evening Post*, 1944.

Bone Key & Other Poems, Aralia Press, West Chester, Pennsylvania, 1997, 180 copies.

For C, broadside, issued on the occasion of a tribute to RW at Amherst College on the fiftieth anniversary of the publication of *The Beautiful Changes*, October 29, 1997, 50 copies.

Signatures, used as a Christmas greeting by the Wilburs, the illustrator, and the publisher, Aralia Press, West Chester, Pennsylvania, 1997, 470 copies.

UNCOLLECTED

'Italy: Maine', *The Saturday Evening Post*, v. 217, no. 12, September 23, 1944. The first line was altered without RW's approval; it was restored to the original wording in a 1997 broadside printing (see above).

'"It is the Time to Reveal Joy"' (part III of 'Notes on Heroes'; part I was 'First Forth Gewat', translated from *Beowulf*; part II was the poem 'Beowulf'), *Wake*, no. 6, Spring, 1948.

'Returning', *'48: The Magazine of the Year*, v. 2, no. 5, May, 1948.

'Natural Song', *The American Scholar*, v. 18, no. 1, winter 1948-49. Reprinted in *American Sampler: a Selection of New Poetry*, ed. Francis Coleman, Prairie Press, Iowa City, Iowa, 1951.

'We', *Poetry*, v. 73, no. 3, December, 1948.

'Tears for the Rich', *American Letters*, v. 1, no. 1 December, 1948.

'Weather Bird', *Poetry*, v. 73, no. 3, December, 1948.

'?' (the question mark is the full title), *American Letters*, v. 1, no. 6, May 1949. Reprinted as facsimile of RW's manuscript in *American Poets Since World War II: Part 2, L-Z*, ed. Donald J. Greiner, Gale, Detroit, Michigan, 1980.

'Western Express', *Glass Hill*, no. 1 October, 1949.

'Nightfalls', *Voices*, no. 136, Winter, 1949.

'A Poem of Dedication for Lincoln Center', in a programme, *Opening Week of Lincoln Center for the Performing Arts*, September 23-30, 1962. Also in *The New York Times*, September 24, 1962.

'A Postcard for Bob Bly', *Kayak*, no. 13, January, 1968.

'Her Hair', lyrics, *Michel Legrand Anthology*, Big 3 Music Corp., New York, 1971.

'Il Disdegnoso', *The New Yorker*, October 7, 1996.

CANDIDE

THE HISTORY OF *CANDIDE*, AND OF THE LYRICS WRITTEN BY RW AT VARIOUS TIMES FOR IT, IS COMPLEX. THE BEST ACCOUNT IS FOUND IN ROBERT A. WILSON'S 'RICHARD WILBUR AND *CANDIDE*', IN *THE PAPERS OF THE BIBLIOGRAPHICAL SOCIETY OF AMERICA*, V. 89, NO. 1 (MARCH 1995), PP. 73-83. THERE HAVE BEEN NUMEROUS RECORDINGS, BOTH VIDEO AND AUDIO, OF VARIOUS PRODUCTIONS. WE HAVE LISTED HERE THOSE PRINTED VERSIONS THAT ARE OF IMPORTANCE FOR DOCUMENTING RW'S CONTRIBUTIONS.

Candide: a Comic Operetta Based on Voltaire's Satire, book by Lillian Hellman, score by Leonard Bernstein, lyrics by RW, other lyrics by John Latouche and Dorothy Parker, Random House, New York, 1957.

Candide: a Comic Operetta Based on Voltaire's Satire, book by Lillian Hellman, music by Leonard Bernstein, lyrics by RW, other lyrics by John Latouche, Dorothy Parker, Lillian Hellman, and Leonard Bernstein, vocal score, G. Schirmer, New York, 1958.

Candide: a Comic Operetta Based on Voltaire's Satire, book by Lillian Hellman, score by Leonard Bernstein, lyrics by RW, other lyrics by John Latouche and Dorothy Parker, Avon (Bard Books, YD14), New York, 1970.

Candide, book adapted from Voltaire by Hugh Wheeler; music by Leonard Bernstein, lyrics by RW, with additional lyrics by Stephen Sondheim and John Latouche, Music Theatre International, New York, 1975.

Candide, music by Leonard Bernstein, book by Hugh Wheeler, adapted from Voltaire, lyrics by RW, John Latouche, and Stephen Sondheim, foreword by Harold Prince, colour photographs by Martha Swope, Schirmer Books, New York, 1976.

Leonard Bernstein, *Candide: A Comic Operetta in Two Acts*, Scottish Opera edition of the opera-house version, 1989. Book by Hugh Wheeler, based on the satire by Voltaire, lyrics by RW, with additional lyrics by Stephen Sondheim, John Latouche, Dorothy Parker, Lillian Hellman and Leonard Bernstein, orchestrations by Leonard Bernstein and Hershey Kay, musical continuity and additional orchestrations by John Mauceri, Jalni Publications, Boosey & Hawkes, New York, 1994. Includes a preface by RW. The texts of this score version first appeared in the libretto accompanying the 1991 set of 2 CDs issued by Deutsche Grammophon, 429 734-2.

TRANSLATIONS

MOST OF RW'S MAJOR BOOKS OF POETRY INCLUDE SOME TRANSLATIONS AS WELL.

MAJOR BOOK PUBLICATIONS

Molière, *The Misanthrope*, Harcourt, Brace and Co., New York, 1955/Faber & Faber, London, 1958/Dramatists Play Service (acting edition), New York, 1989

Molière, *Tartuffe*, Harcourt, Brace & World, New York, 1963/Faber & Faber, London, 1964/ Dramatists Play Service (acting edition), New York, 1989?/Harcourt, Brace and Co., (bilingual edition), New York, 1997.

Molière, *The Misanthrope and Tartuffe*, Harcourt, Brace & World, New York, 1965.
Molière, *The School for Wives*, Dramatists Play Service (acting edition), New York, 1971/ Harcourt Brace Jovanovich (trade edition), New York, 1971.
Molière, *The Learned Ladies*, Dramatists Play Service (acting edition), New York, 1977/ Harcourt Brace Jovanovich (trade edition), New York and London, 1978/as *Les femmes savantes*, Hippocrene Books (bilingual edition), New York, 1997.
Molière, *Four Comedies*, reprints the four separate works by Molière listed above, Harcourt Brace Jovanovich, New York and London, 1982.
Racine, *Andromache*, Harcourt Brace Jovanovich (trade edition), San Diego, New York and London, 1982/Dramatists Play Service (acting edition), New York, 1982.
The Whale and Other Uncollected Translations, BOA Editions, Brockport, New York, 1982.
Racine, *Phaedra*, Harcourt Brace Jovanovich (trade edition), San Diego, New York, and London, 1986/Dramatists Play Service (acting edition), New York, 1987.
Molière, *The School for Husbands*, Dramatists Play Service (acting edition), New York, 1991/ Harcourt Brace Jovanovich (trade edition), New York, San Diego, London, 1992.
Molière, *The Imaginary Cuckold, or Sganarelle*, Dramatists Play Service (acting edition), New York, 1993.
Molière, *The School for Husbands; and, Sganarelle, or The Imaginary Cuckold*, Harcourt, Brace and Co., San Diego, New York, London, 1993 (in fact, 1994).
Molière, *Amphitryon*, Dramatists Play Service (acting edition), New York, 1995/Harcourt, Brace and Co., (trade edition), New York, San Diego, London, 1995).
Molière, *Don Juan*, Dramatists Play Service (acting edition), New York, 1998, Harcourt, (trade edition), New York, San Diego, London, forthcoming, Fall, 2000.
Molière, *The Bungler*, Dramatists Play Service (acting edition), New York, 2000.

LIMITED EDITION, PRIVATE PRESS, PERSONAL, BROADSIDE, AND SIMILAR PUBLICATIONS

Jean Sarment, *The Children's Playhouse*, mimeographed playscript, 1957?
Anna Akhmatova, *Lot's Wife*, the Wilburs' Christmas card, 1962.
The Pelican, from a Bestiary of 1120, printed for Philip Hofer, Stanbrook Abbey Press, England, 1963, 450 copies.
Joseph Brodsky, *The Funeral of Bobò*, broadside, Artis, (n.p.), 1974, about 200 copies.
Jean Racine, *Andromache Speaks to Pyrrhus*, a 'Chimera Broadside', Matrix Press, Palo Alto, California, 1982, 50 copies. From Act III, scene 6, of *Andromache*.
Vinicius de Moraes, *Song*, postcard advertisement for *The Whale*, BOA Editions, Brockport, New York, 1982, about 500 copies. Also printed as part of an advertising flyer.
Voltaire, 'To Madame du Châtelet', together with the original and a version by Ezra Pound, in a handout for a talk by RW at Amherst College, May 28, 1992, 200 copies.

UNCOLLECTED

Villiers de L'Isle Adam, 'The Swan-Killer', *Quarterly Review of Literature*, v. 4, no. 1,1947.
Yevgeni Yevtushenko, 'Light Died in the Hall ...' (erroneously entitled 'Stolen Apples'), *West Coast Poetry Review*, v. 1, no. 1, Summer, 1971. Reprinted in, Yevgeni Yevtushenko, *Stolen Apples*, Doubleday, Garden City, New York, 1971.
André Gide, 'Persephone', *Choreography by George Balanchine: A Catalogue of Works*. Eakins Press Foundation, New York, 1983. Final four lines only.
Georgi Djagarov, 'Elegy', *Poets of Bulgaria*, ed. William Meredith, Unicorn Press, Greensboro, North Carolina, 1986.
Badawi al-Jabal, 'Dark Mirage', *Modern Arabic Poetry*, ed. Salma Khadra Jayyusi, Columbia

University Press, New York, 1987.

Valeri Petrov, 'Calm', 'A Cry from Childhood', 'Jewish Jokes', and 'Photos from the Archives', *Window on the Black Sea: Bulgarian Poetry in Translation*, ed. Richard Harteis, Carnegie Mellon University Press, Pittsburgh, Pennsylvania, 1992. The second and fourth are collected in *Mayflies*.

Dante, Canto XXV in *Dante's Inferno: Translations by Twenty Contemporary Poets* (trade edition and limited signed edition of 145 copies), Ecco Press, Hopewell, New Jersey, 1993.

PROSE

MAJOR BOOK PUBLICATIONS

Responses, Harcourt Brace Jovanovich, New York and London, 1976. Reprinted, with additional material, Story Line Press, Ashland, Oregon, 2000.

The Catbird's Song, Harcourt Brace and Co., New York, San Diego, London, 1997.

LIMITED EDITION, PRIVATE PRESS, PERSONAL, BROADSIDE, AND SIMILAR PUBLICATIONS

History of the 36th Signal Company, Message Center Section, in France, Germany, and Austria, August 15, 1944–May 8, 1945, Kaufbeuren, Germany, 1945, about 50 copies.

An Address Given at the Dedication of the Robert Frost Library, Amherst College, mimeographed from typescript, 24 October, 1965. Includes the poem 'Seed Leaves'.

Elizabeth Bishop: A Memorial Tribute, Albondocani Press, New York, 1982, 174 numbered and 26 lettered copies in wrappers, 12 hard-cover copies with photographic frontispiece.

On My Own Work, Aquila Publishing Co., Portree, Isle of Skye, Scotland, 1983. Prepared for the Voice of America in the 1970s. Reprinted without RW's knowledge or involvement. Includes the text of three poems.

'Poetry's Debt to Poetry', broadside, the text of *Washington College Literary Award Presented to Richard Wilbur, March 25, 1988*, 250 copies.

About Wallace Stevens, postcard, Literary House Press, Chestertown, Maryland, 1994, 500 copies.

The 1996 Frost Medal Lecture, Poetry Society of America, New York, 1997 (in fact, 1998), 120 copies.

UNCOLLECTED

'The Day after the War', *Foreground*, v. 1, no. 2, Spring/Summer, 1946.

Autobiographical Note, *Ten Poets Anthology*, ed. Anthony Harrigan, East Dorset, Vermont, 1947.

Comments on RW's poems 'Driftwood' and 'To an American Poet Just Dead', *Poetry: A Critical Supplement*, December, 1948.

'Between Visits', review of C. Day Lewis, *Poems 1943-1947*, *Poetry*, v. 74, no. 2, May, 1949.

'The Genie in the Bottle', responses to a questionnaire, *Mid-Century American Poets*, ed. John Ciardi, Twayne, New York, 1950.

Review of N. Bryllion Fagin, *The Histrionic Mr. Poe*, *The New England Quarterly*, v. 23, no. 1, March, 1950.

'English 271. Edgar Allan Poe', course description, *Official Register of Harvard University*, v. 47, no. 23, September, 1950.

Untitled, in a section entitled 'Statements by Friends and Associates', *Monthly Review*, v. 2, no. 6, October, 1950. Reprinted in *F. O. Matthiessen (1902-1950): A Collective Portrait*, ed. Paul M. Sweezy and Leo Huberman, Henry Schuman, New York, 1950.

Review of John Frederick Nims, *A Fountain in Kentucky and Other Poems*, *Poetry*, v. 77, no. 2, November, 1950.

'Seven Poets', review of William Empson, *Collected Poems*, D. H. Lawrence, *The Selected Poems*, William Carlos Williams, *The Selected Poems*, Elizabeth Daryush, *Selected Poems*, John Heath-Stubbs, *The Charity of the Stars*, Hyam Plutzik, *Aspects of Proteus*, and James Broughton, *The Playground*, *Sewanee Review*, v. 58, no. 2, Winter, 1950. The portion on Empson was reprinted in *Critical Essays on William Empson*, ed. John Constable, Scolar Press, Aldershot, Hampshire, 1993.

Review of William Van O'Connor, *The Shaping Spirit: A Study of Wallace Stevens*, *The New England Quarterly*, v. 24, no. 1, March, 1951.

Review of *The Oxford Book of American Verse*, ed. F. O. Matthiessen, *The New England Quarterly*, v. 24, no. 1, March, 1951.

'English S-278c. Modern Poetry: American Poets Since 1900 with Some Study of their British Contemporaries', course description, *Official Register of Harvard University*, v. 48, no. 10, May, 1951.

'Inclusive View', review of W. H. Auden, *Nones*, *The Hopkins Review*, v. 5, no. 1, Fall, 1951.

Letter to the Secretary of the Amherst College Class of 1942, *Amherst Alumni News*, v. 5, no. 3, December, 1952.

Review of Archibald MacLeish, *Collected Poems: 1917-1952*, *The New England Quarterly*, v. 26, no. 1, March, 1953.

'The Problem of Creative Thinking in Poetry', *The Nature of Creative Thinking*, Industrial Research Institute, New York, 1953.

'Translator's Note', accompanying RW's translation of Francis Jammes's 'A Prayer to Go to Paradise with the Donkeys', *Furioso*, v. 8, no. 1, Spring, 1953.

'Urgency and Artifice', review of Barbara Howes, *In the Cold Country*, and Anthony Hecht, *A Summoning of Stones*, *The New York Times Book Review*, April 4, 1974. The review of Howes was excerpted in *Contemporary Literary Criticism*, v. 15, ed. Sharon R. Gunton and Laurie Lanzen Harris, Gale, Detroit, Michigan, 1980.

Autobiographical Note, *Twentieth Century Authors: First Supplement*, ed. Stanley J. Kunitz, H. W. Wilson, New York, 1955.

'[English] 210 (1), (2). Modern Poetry', course description, *Wellesley College Bulletin*, v. 45, no. 2, October 20, 1955. Course taught with David Ferry.

'[English] 202 (1). Poetry', course description, *Wellesley College Bulletin*, v. 45, no. 2, October 20, 1955.

Review of Robert Graves, *Collected Poems 1955*, *Poetry*, v. 87, no. 3, December, 1955.

Comments on Ezra Pound, as part of a symposium, *Nuova Corrente*, no. 5-6, January-June, 1956.

'California World', review of Josephine Miles, *Prefabrications*, *The Saturday Review*, v. 39, no. 7, February 18, 1956.

Introduction to RW's translation of René Char, 'Les Transparents', *Poetry*, v. 87, no. 6, March, 1956.

'The Heart of the Thing', review of Marianne Moore, *Like a Bulwark*, *The New York Times Book Review*, November 11, 1956.

'Poetry and Landscape', Gyorgy Kepes, *The New Landscape in Art and Science*, Paul Theobald and Co., Chicago, Illinois, 1956.

Letter to the Secretary of the Amherst College Class of 1942, *Amherst Alumni News*, v. 9, no. 4, April, 1957.

'Campaign Fodder', letter to the editor, *Worcester Telegram*, Worcester, Massachusetts, May 4, 1957.

'English 8. Verse Writing', course description, *Wesleyan University Bulletin*, v. 51, no. 3, October, 1957.

'Commentary', part of a symposium on RW's poem, 'Love Calls Us to the Things of this World', *The Berkeley Review*, v. 1, no. 3, Fall/Winter? 1957. Reprinted in *The Contemporary Poet as Artist and Critic*, ed. Anthony Ostroff, Little, Brown, Boston, Massachusetts,1964.

'English 51. Senior Seminar: Poetry', course description, *Wesleyan University Bulletin*, v. 52, no. 3, October, 1958.

'Presentation to Robert Graves of the Russell Loines Award for Poetry', *Proceedings of the American Academy of Arts and Letters and the National Institute of Arts and Letters*, 2nd series, no. 9, 1959.

Review of F. O. Matthiessen, *The Achievement of T. S. Eliot: An Essay on the Nature of Poetry; with a chapter on Eliot's later work by C. L. Barber*, 3rd edition, *Amherst Alumni News*, v. 11, no. 3, January, 1959.

'And No Place to Call Home', review of Yvan Goll, *Jean Sans Terre*, *The New York Times Book Review*, January 4, 1959.

'English 46. Modern Poetry', course description, *Wesleyan University Bulletin*, v. 53, no. 3, October, 1959.

'The House of Poe', *Anniversary Lectures 1959*, Library of Congress, Washington, D.C.,1959.

Citations for Stanley Kunitz and James Wright, *Proceedings of the American Academy of Arts and Letters and the National Institute of Arts and Letters*, 2nd series, no. 10, 1960.

'Commencement Address', in *Commencement, Lawrence College, June 1960*.

'Presentation to Abbie Huston Evans of the Russell Loines Award for Poetry', *Proceedings of the American Academy of Arts and Letters and the National Institute of Arts and Letters*, 2nd series, no. 11, 1961. Excerpted in Abbie Huston Evans, *Fact of Crystal*, Harcourt, Brace & Co., New York, 1961.

Introduction to RW's translation of Molière, *Tartuffe*, Act I, scenes 2-5, *Poetry*, v. 98, no. 6, September, 1961.

'English 63. Senior Seminar: Poetry', course description, *Wesleyan University Bulletin*, v. 55, no. 3, September, 1961.

'Two Chard Dishes', Beryl Barr and Barbara Turner Sachs, *The Artists' & Writers' Cookbook*, Contact Editions, Sausalito, California, 1961.

Essay included in a symposium, 'The Poet and His Critics, III: A Symposium on Robert Lowell's "Skunk Hour"', ed. Anthony Ostroff, *New World Writing 21*, 1962. Reprinted in *The Contemporary Poet as Artist and Critic*, ed. Anthony Ostroff, Little, Brown, Boston, Massachusetts,1964.

'Poems that Soar and Sing and Charm', review of Robert Frost, *In the Clearing*, *New York Herald Tribune Books*, March 25, 1962. Reprinted in *Robert Frost: The Critical Reception*, ed. Linda W. Wagner, Burt Franklin, New York, 1977. Also on the CD, *Robert Frost: Poems, Life, Legacy*, noted below under video recordings.

Comments on Robert Hillyer, *Venture*, May, 1962.

'English 23. Milton', course description, *Wesleyan University Bulletin*, v. 56, no. 2, September, 1962.

Comment on RW's poem, 'A Baroque Wall-Fountain in the Villa Sciarra', *Poet's Choice*, ed. Paul Engle and Joseph Langland, Dial Press, New York, 1962.

Introduction to RW's translation of Molière, *Tartuffe*, Act IV, *The Massachusetts Review*, v. 4, no. 3, Spring, 1963.

'An Afterword' to *New Writing from Virginia*, ed. George Garrett, New Writing Associates, Charlottesville, Virginia, 1963.

'English 63. Junior-Senior Seminar: Poe', course description, *Wesleyan University Bulletin*, v. 57, no. 2, September, 1963.

Entry on Poe, *The Concise Encyclopedia of English and American Poets and Poetry*, ed. Stephen Spender and Donald Hall, Hutchinson, London/Hawthorn Books, New York, 1963.

'Seminariet en Succé', *Horisont*, v. 11, no. 4, 1964, in Swedish.

Response to a question about the economics of writing included in 'Writers and $$$$$$$$', *Contact*, v. 4, no. 4, issue no. 18, April/May, 1964.

Introduction of speakers, *National Poetry Festival: Proceedings*, Library of Congress, Washington, D.C., 1964.

Letter to the Secretary of the Amherst College Class of 1942, *Amherst Alumni News*, v. 17, no. 2, Fall, 1964.

'119R American Poetry', course description, *Wesleyan University Bulletin*, v. 59, no. 2, September, 1965.

'An Open Letter', signed by 120 others, deploring the conviction and sentencing of Andrei Sinyavsky and Yuri Daniel in the USSR, *Partisan Review*, v. 33, no. 2, Spring, 1966.

Untitled, William L. Martz, *The Distinctive Voice*, Scott, Foresman and Co., Glenview, Illinois, 1966.

'Richard Wilbur Replies', to Tom Burns Haber's letter to the editor, *The New York Review of Books*, v. 8, no. 9, May 18, 1967.

'Richard Wilbur Replies', to Norman N. Holland's letter to the editor, *The New York Review of Books*, v. 9, no. 4, September 14, 1967.

Untitled, *Authors Take Sides on Vietnam*, ed. Cecil Woolf and John Bagguley, Simon and Schuster, New York, 1967. RW's contribution was not included in the English edition of the work.

'A Public Statement on Soviet Jewry', signed by approximately 200 others, *The New York Review of Books*, v. 9, no. 11, December 21, 1967.

Citation for A. R. Ammons, *Proceedings of the American Academy of Arts and Letters and the National Institute of Arts and Letters*, 2nd series, no. 18, 1968. RW wrote only the descriptive last portion of the sentence.

Response to a questionnaire on the state of translation, *Delos*, no. 2, 1968.

Open letter about 'Vietnam Commencements', signed by 11 others, *The New Republic*, v. 158, no. 16, April 20, 1968.

Letter, reproduced from RW's manuscript, as an advertisement with a list of the Committee of Arts and Letters for Humphrey-Muskie, *The New York Times*, October 27, 1968.

Comments on the production of his translation of Molière's *Tartuffe*, in a letter to Peter Raby, *The Stratford Scene 1958-1968*, ed. Peter Raby, Clarke, Irwin & Co., Toronto, 1968.

Letter to the Secretary of the Amherst College Class of 1942, *Amherst Alumni News*, v. 23, no. 1, Summer, 1970.

Untitled, *Contemporary Poets of the English Language*, ed. Rosalie Murphy, St. James Press, Chicago and London, 1970.

'205 Milton', course description, *Wesleyan University Bulletin*, v. 64, no. 2, September, 1970.

Introduction to RW's poem, 'Walking to Sleep', *This is My Best in the Third Quarter of the Century*, ed. Whit Burnett, Doubleday, Garden City, New York, 1970.

Untitled, John P. Field, *Richard Wilbur: A Bibliographical Checklist*, Kent State University Press, Kent, Ohio, 1971.

Letter to the Secretary of the Amherst College Class of 1942, *Amherst Alumni News*, v. 23, no. 4, Spring, 1971.

'267 PT American Poetry', course description, *Wesleyan University Bulletin*, v. 65, no. 2,

September, 1971.
Untitled, *Attacks of Taste*, ed. Evelyn B. Byrne and Otto M. Penzler, Gotham Book Mart, New York, 1971.
Untitled, William Jay Smith, *Louise Bogan: A Woman's Words*, Library of Congress, Washington, D.C., 1971.
Memorial of Peter Boynton, *Peter*, ed. Arthur Wensinger, Gehenna Press, Northampton, Massachusetts, 1972.
Contribution to a symposium, 'The State of Poetry', *The Review*, no. 29-30, Spring/Summer, 1972.
'269 PT Poe', course description, *Wesleyan University Bulletin*, v. 66, no. 2, September, 1972.
Introduction to 'Some Opposites', *The Denver Quarterly*, v. 7, no. 4, Winter, 1973.
Introductions to readings of several of RW's poems and translations, *Proceedings of the American Academy of Arts and Letters and the National Institute of Arts and Letters*, 2nd series, no. 23, 1973.
'Ford's Better Idea', letter to the editor, *The New York Review of Books*, v. 19, no. 11/12, January 25, 1973.
Comment on reading, *The Reading Teacher*, v. 26, no. 6, March, 1973.
'267 American Poetry', course description, *Wesleyan University Bulletin*, v. 67, no. 2, August, 1973.
Letter to the Soviet Ambassador to the U.S., Anatoly Dobrynin, from RW and three others, *American PEN Newsletter*, no. 10, December, 1973.
Contribution to a series, 'Authors on Translators', *Translation*, v. 2, no. 1/2, Winter, 1974.
'Opposites', an introduction to the printing of some of them, *Cricket*, v. 1, no. 7, March, 1974.
'217 PT Milton', course description, *Wesleyan University Bulletin*, v. 68, no. 1, August, 1974.
'167 PT Verse Writing', course description, *Wesleyan University Bulletin*, v. 68, no. 1, August, 1974.
'Tribute' to Francis Ponge, *Books Abroad*, v. 48, no. 4, Autumn, 1974.
'267 PT American Poetry', course description, *Wesleyan University Bulletin*, v. 69, no. 1, August, 1975.
'Herb Vinegar', *John Keats's Porridge: Favorite Recipes of American Poets*, University of Iowa Press, Iowa City, Iowa, 1975.
'Opening of the Ceremonial and Announcement of Newly Elected Honorary Members of the Academy-Institute by Richard Wilbur, President of the Academy', distributed in a press release at the Ceremonial, May 21, 1975, then printed in *Proceedings of the American Academy of Arts and Letters and the National Institute of Arts and Letters*, 2nd series, no. 26, 1976.
'Induction of New Members of the Academy by the President of the Academy', *Proceedings of the American Academy of Arts and Letters and the National Institute of Arts and Letters*, 2nd series, no. 26, 1976.
Introduction to 'The Blashfield Foundation Address' delivered by Stephen Spender, *Proceedings of the American Academy of Arts and Letters and the National Institute of Arts and Letters*, 2nd series, no. 26, 1976.
'Music, Sound, Tone, and the Poetry of Frost: a Conversation' between RW and Cleanth Brooks, moderated by Jack L. Nelson, *Robert Frost Read and Remembered*, ed. Margaret G. Trotter, Agnes Scott College, Decatur, Georgia, 1976.
'269 PT Poe', course description, *Wesleyan University Bulletin*, v. 70, no. 1, July, 1976.
'171 PT Verse Writing', course description, *Wesleyan University Bulletin*, v. 70, no. 1, July, 1976.
Self-portrait and untitled statement about it, Burt Britton, *Self-Portrait*, Random House, New

York, 1976.

'Opening of the Ceremonial and Announcement of Newly Elected Honorary Members of the Academy-Institute by Richard Wilbur, President of the Academy', *Proceedings of the American Academy of Arts and Letters and the National Institute of Arts and Letters*, 2nd series, no. 27, 1977.

'Induction of New Members of the Academy by the President of the Academy', *Proceedings of the American Academy of Arts and Letters and the National Institute of Arts and Letters*, 2nd series, no. 27, 1977.

Introduction to 'The Blashfield Foundation Address' delivered by Henry Steele Commager, distributed in a press release at the Ceremonial, May 19, 1976, then printed in *Proceedings of the American Academy of Arts and Letters and the National Institute of Arts and Letters*, 2nd series, no. 27, 1977.

Introduction to RW's translation of act III, scenes 1-3, of Molière's *The Learned Ladies*, *Shenandoah*, v. 28, no. 3, Spring, 1977.

'For Better or for Worse', *Mississippi Review*, v.6, no. 1, Spring, May, 1971.

Letter to Alberta Turner, *50 Contemporary Poets: The Creative Process*, ed. Alberta T. Turner, David McKay Co., New York, 1977.

'260a Writing Poetry', course description, *Smith College Bulletin*, v. 71, no. 3, September, 1977.

'Tartuffe: Ruthless, Bullying, Evil – and Human', *The New York Times*, September 25, 1977 (section 2).

Untitled, about Wilbert Snow, *Hermes*, v. 4, no. 3, October 20, 1977, in a section entitled *Hermes Literary Supplement*.

'The Poetry of Witter Bynner', *The American Poetry Review*, v. 6, no. 6, November/December, 1977.

'Poems: Experience Expressed Truly and Well', *Journal of Autism and Childhood Schizophrenia*, v. 7, no. 4, December, 1977.

Introduction to RW's translation of act IV, scene 2, of Molière's *The Learned Ladies*, *A Review*, Amherst, Massachusetts, v. 5, December, 1977.

'Induction of New Honorary Members of the Academy-Institute by the Chancellor of the Academy', distributed in a press release at the Ceremonial, May 18, 1977, then printed in *Proceedings of the American Academy of Arts and Letters and the National Institute of Arts and Letters*, 2nd series, no. 28, 1978.

'Misanthrope Mishap', *The New York Review of Books*, v. 24, no. 21/22, January 26, 1978.

'The Learned Ladies', an introduction to RW's translation of excerpts from acts I-II of Molière's *The Learned Ladies*, *Translation*, v. 5, Spring, 1978.

Comment on the poetry of Thomas Whitbread, *Lucille*, no. 10, Summer, 1978.

'339a American Literature. Topic for 1978-79: Edgar Allan Poe', course description, *Smith College Bulletin*, v. 72, no. 3, September, 1978.

Comment on RW's story, 'A Game of Catch', Edmund J. Farrell et al., *Arrangement in Literature*, Scott, Foresman and Co., Glenview, Illinois, 1979 [in fact, 1978].

Untitled, LaVerne H. Clark, *Focus 101*, Heidelberg Graphics, Chico, California, 1979.

'From Key West Florida', about Wallace Stevens, *The Wallace Stevens Journal*, v. 3, no. 3/4, Fall, 1979.

'Boycott TABA', letter to the editor, signed by 44 others, expressing concern over the proposal to have publishers rather than writers serving as judges for The American Book Awards programme, *The New York Review of Books*, v. 26, no. 15, October 11, 1979.

'La Fontaine in English', review of La Fontaine, *Selected Fables*, trans. James Michie, and *Some Tales of La Fontaine*, trans. C. H. Sisson, *The New York Times Book Review*, October 14, 1979.

'Presentation to Archibald MacLeish of the Gold Medal for Poetry', distributed in a press release at the Ceremonial, May 23, 1979, then printed in *Proceedings of the American*

Academy of Arts and Letters and the National Institute of Arts and Letters, 2nd series, no. 30, 1980.

Untitled, on I. A. Richards's poetry, *PN Review,* v. 7, no. 2, issue no. 16, 1980.

Foreword to Susan Donovan, *The White Lobster,* Blue Willow Inn Press, Northampton, Massachusetts, 1980.

'The Life of Molière', *TV Guide,* v. 26, no. 2, issue 1398, January 12, 1980.

Excerpts from a letter, *Catalogue Seventeen,* Joseph the Provider (bookseller), 1980.

'Commentary', *Dreamworks,* v. 1, no. 2, Summer, 1980.

Autobiographical note, *Contemporary Poets,* ed. James Vinson, St. Martin's Press, New York/Macmillan, London, 1980.

'New England's Brooks', *New England: The Four Seasons,* ed. Arthur Griffin, Houghton Mifflin, Boston, Massachusetts, 1980.

Untitled, *Richard Eberhart: A Celebration,* ed. Sydney Lea et al., New England Review, Kenyon Hill Publications, Hanover, New Hampshire, 1980.

Untitled, in a section entitled 'The Educational Program', *There's Never Been a Better Time than Now,* The Campaign for Amherst, Amherst, Massachusetts, 1980.

'Induction of New Honorary Members of the Academy-Institute by Richard Wilbur, Chancellor of the Academy', distributed in a press release at the Ceremonial, May 20, 1980, then printed in *Proceedings of the American Academy of Arts and Letters and the National Institute of Arts and Letters,* 2nd series, no. 31, 1981.

'Induction of New Members of the Academy-Institute by the Chancellor of the Academy', distributed in a press release at the Ceremonial, May 20, 1980, then printed in *Proceedings of the American Academy of Arts and Letters and the National Institute of Arts and Letters,* 2nd series, no. 31, 1981.

Notes on several of RW's poems, *The Harper Anthology of Poetry,* ed. John Frederick Nims, Harper and Row, New York, 1981.

Excerpts from letters to Paul Auster (June 3 & 13, 1980) about RW's translation of Guillaume Apollinaire's 'Le Pont Mirabeau', *Modern Poetry in Translation,* no. 41/42, March, 1981.

Recipe for sorrel fish sauce, *The Great American Writers' Cookbook,* ed. Dean Faulkner Wells, Yoknapatawpha Press, Oxford, Mississippi, 1981.

Review of Hjalmar Gullberg, *Gentleman, Single, Refined,* translated by Judith Moffett, *Scandinavian Review,* v. 69, no. 4, December, 1981.

Letter about a tribute to James Laughlin, *Conjunctions,* no. 1, Winter, 1981-82.

'Poe and the Art of Suggestion', *The University of Mississippi Studies in English,* n.s. v. 3, 1982.

'Open Letter to Readership of the American Poetry Review' about the civil war in El Salvador, signed by 125 others, *The American Poetry Review,* v. 11, no. 3, May/June, 1982.

'Richard Wilbur, Lake Forest College Commencement Speaker', reprints RW's address, *Congressional Record,* v. 128, no. 63, May 21, 1982.

'220a Milton', course description, *Smith College Bulletin,* v. 76, no. 3, September, 1982.

Foreword to Thomas Whitbread, *Whomp and Moonshiver,* BOA Editions, Brockport, New York, 1982.

'At a Certain Remove', part of a symposium, 'The Writer's Role: Responses to Hortense Calisher', *The New Criterion,* v. 1, no. 6, February, 1983.

Comment on RW's poem, 'A Mill', *Poetspeak: In Their Work, About Their Work,* ed. Paul B. Janeczko, Bradbury Press, Scarsdale, New York, 1983.

Introduction to Robert Francis, *Butter Hill,* Paul W. Carman, Springfield, Massachusetts, 1984.

'Terror Wasn't His Only Talent', review of *Edgar Allan Poe: Essays and Reviews,* ed. G. R. Thompson, *The New York Times Book Review,* September 9, 1984.

'A Tribute' to Lillian Hellman, *Dictionary of Literary Biography Yearbook 1984,* ed. Jean W. Ross, Gale, Detroit, Michigan, 1985.

Excerpt from a letter to Peter Stitt, Peter Stitt, *The World's Hieroglyphic Beauty,* University of

Georgia Press, Athens, Georgia, 1985.

Comments in an article by John F. Andrews, 'Taylor-Made Shakespeare? Or is "Shall I die?" the long-lost text of Bottom's dream?' *Dictionary of Literary Biography Yearbook 1985*, ed. Jean W. Ross, Gale, Detroit, Michigan, 1986.

Foreword to *Archibald MacLeish: Reflections*, ed. Bernard A. Drabeck and Helen E. Ellis, University of Massachusetts Press, Amherst, Massachusetts, 1986.

'A Letter to Ada', *The Proceedings of the Archibald MacLeish Symposium, May 7-8, 1982*, ed. Bernard A. Drabeck and Helen E. Ellis, University Press of America, Lanham, Maryland, 1988.

Comments in 'Close-Up: Richard Wilbur, 1987 Poet Laureate', by Judson Jerome, Judson Jerome, *1989 Poet's Market*, Writers Digest Books, Cincinnati, Ohio, 1988.

Untitled, *The Best American Poetry 1988*, ed. John Ashbery, Collier, New York, 1988.

'Hoaxing Motives Vary: Greed, Pride, Power, Fun', *The Lewis Legacy: Newsletter of the C. S. Lewis Foundation for Truth in Publishing*, no. 12, July, 1989.

Portion of a letter, Kathryn Lindskoog, *Creative Writing for People Who Can't Not Write*, Academie Books, Zondervan Publishing House, Grand Rapids, Michigan, 1989.

Correspondence and 'Postscript: Wilbur to Weissbort', *Translating Poetry: The Double Labyrinth*, ed. Daniel Weissbort, University of Iowa Press, Iowa City, Iowa, 1989.

Introduction to *'Lives of Works that Matter': A Catalogue of Inscribed Books, Letters and Manuscripts*, Randy F. Weinstein, Bookseller, Southfield, Massachusetts, 1989.

Acceptance speech, *The National Book Award: Writers on Their Craft and Their World*, Book-of-the-Month Club, New York, 1990.

'A Tribute' to Robert Penn Warren, *Dictionary of Literary Biography Yearbook, 1989*, ed. J. M. Brock, Gale, Detroit, Michigan, 1990.

Comment on RW's poem 'A Wall in the Woods: Cummington', *The Best American Poetry 1990*, ed. Jorie Graham, Scribner, New York, 1990.

'The Initial Response', a reply to the question 'What's the first thing that comes into your head when you hear the name Emily Dickinson?', *The Single Hound*, v. 2, no. 2, December, 1990.

Citation for James Merrill, *Proceedings of the American Academy and Institute of Arts and Letters*, 2nd series, no. 41, 1990, ©1991.

'May Swenson, 1919-1989', *Proceedings of the American Academy and Institute of Arts and Letters*, 2nd series, no. 41, 1990, ©1991.

Foreword to Frances Bixler, *Richard Wilbur: A Reference Guide*, G. K. Hall, Boston, Massachusetts, 1991.

Portion of a letter to Bruce Michelson, *Wilbur's Poetry: Music in a Scattering Time*, University of Massachusetts Press, Amherst, Massachusetts, 1991.

'Greetings from Richard Wilbur', *Shorelines*, v. 1, no. 1, Fall/Winter, 1991.

Foreword to Rollie McKenna, *A Life in Photography*, Knopf, New York, 1991.

Gold Medal acceptance speech, *Proceedings of the American Academy and Institute of Arts and Letters*, 2nd series, no. 42, 1992.

Autobiographical note, *Amherst College 1942*, Class of 1942 Reunion book, Amherst, Massachusetts, 1992.

'A Happy Conjunction', *The Poetry of Song: Five Tributes to Stephen Sondheim*, ed. George Robert Minkoff and J. D. McClatchy, Poetry Society of America, New York, 1992.

Speech accepting Edward MacDowell Medal, *MacDowell Colony News*, v. 21, no. 2, Fall/Winter, 1992-93. Excerpted in *Medal Day at the MacDowell Colony*, MacDowell Colony, Peterborough, New Hampshire, 1994.

Tribute to Seamus Heaney on his induction as an Honorary Foreign Member, *Proceedings of the American Academy and Institute of Arts and Letters*, 2nd series, no. 44, 1993.

Portion of a letter to 'Eleanor', *List 93-C*, George Robert Minkoff Rare Books, 1993.

'Delightful Poems of Love and Sexual Joy', review of *The Love Poems of May Swenson*,

Solares Hill, v. 17, no. 27, March 11, 1993.

'Stephen Dunn's Poetry is a Great Wonder', review of Stephen Dunn, *Landscape at the End of the Century*, *Solares Hill*, v. 17, no. 28, March 25, 1993.

Letter to Lillian Hellman, reproduced in facsimile, *The Library Chronicle of the University of Texas at Austin*, v. 25, no. 1, 1994.

Preface to Richard Moore, *The Rule that Liberates*, University of South Dakota Press, Vermillion, South Dakota, 1994.

Remarks accepting a medal from the National Arts Club, *PSA News: Newsletter of the Poetry Society of America*, v. 44 & 45, Autumn, 1994.

'Degas and Transcendence', *Tranforming Vision: Writers on Art*, ed. Edward Hirsch, Art Institute of Chicago, Chicago, Illinois/Little, Brown, Boston, Massachusetts, 1994.

'A Letter', *A Glass of Green Tea – With Honig*, ed. Susan Brown et al., Alephoe Books, Providence, Rhode Island, 1994.

Comments on the choice of a sonnet by Sarah Birnbaum for the Howard Nemerov Sonnet Award, in 'Editor's Note', *The Formalist*, v. 5, no. 2, November, 1994.

Untitled remarks about RW's work, *Poem for the Day*, ed. Nicholas Albery, Sinclair-Stevenson, London, 1994. Published in the U.S., with some different poems, as *A Poem a Day*, ed. Karen McCosker and Nicholas Albery, Steerforth Press, South Royalton, Vermont, 1994.

'A Deprivation for All Concerned', in 'The Humanities: in Memoriam', proceedings of a symposium, 'A Humanities and Arts Memorial', *Academic Questions*, v. 8, no. 1, Winter, 1994-95.

'The Death of a Poet', memorial remarks about James Merrill, *Solares Hill*, v. 19, no. 6, February 9, 1995. Reprinted in *JM: A Remembrance*, ed. Robin Magowan and Mark Magowan, Academy of American Poets, New York, 1996.

Untitled, *Paul Horgan, 1 August 1903-7 March 1995*, keepsake of a memorial service held at Wesleyan University, April 29, 1995.

'Poet Laureate Richard Wilbur on "Finchley Avenue"', *The Lewis Legacy: Newsletter of the C.S. Lewis Foundation for Truth in Publishing*, no. 65, Summer, 1995.

Letter to Malcolm Hunter, December 2, 1994, in a programme for the production of *Candide* at the Gulbenkian Theatre, University of Kent, June 27-July 1, 1995.

'An Appreciation', *Constance Stuart Larrabee: Time Exposure*, catalogue of an exhibition, Yale Center for British Art, New Haven, Connecticut, 1995.

Foreword to *A Year in Poetry*, ed. Thomas E. Foster and Elizabeth C. Guthrie, Crown, New York, 1995. The initial publication, in the hard-cover printing, contained an error, which was corrected in the paperback printing of the same year.

Correspondence with Rachel MacKenzie, *The Dark Horse*, no. 2, December, 1995.

'On Formalism, Translation, and Beloved Books of Childhood', *Black Warrior*, v. 22, no. 2 Spring/Summer, 1996.

Preface to *Sixty Years of American Poetry: Celebrating the Anniversary of the Academy of American Poets*, ed. Bruno Navsky and Ellen Rosefsky Cohen, Harry N. Abrams, New York, 1996.

Untitled, *F. Scott Fitzgerald at 100: Centenary Tributes by American Writers*, ed. Patricia Ahearn, Quill & Brush, Rockville, Maryland, 1996.

Excerpts from 'The Frost Medal Reading and Talk', *Journal of the Poetry Society of America*, no. 48, Autumn, 1996.

Foreword to R. R. Knudsen and Suzanne Bigelow, *May Swenson: A Poet's Life in Photos*, Logan, Utah State University Press, Utah, 1996.

Two letters, *Meter in English: A Critical Engagement*, ed. David Baker, University of Arkansas Press, Fayetteville, Arkansas, 1996.

Comments on children's literature, *Once Upon a Time ...: Children's Literature in the Late 20th Century*, programme for the 16th Annual Key West Literary Seminar, Key West, Florida, January 8-11, 1998.

Introduction of a reading by Timothy Steele, *Newsletter of the Friends of the Amherst College Library*, v. 23, 1996-1997.

'Good Manners, Good Literature', acceptance speech for the 1996 T. S. Eliot Award for Creative Writing, *Chronicles*, September, 1997.

Comments on Edgar Allan Poe, *Poets on Poets*, ed. Nick Rennison and Michael Schmidt, Carcanet Press, Manchester, in association with Waterstone's, 1997.

'John Malcolm Brinnin (September 13, 1916 – June 25, 1998)', *Solares Hill*, v. 21, no. 27, July 2, 1998.

Response to 'What's American about American Poetry?' and an entry under 'First Loves (part IV)', *Journal of the Poetry Society of America*, no. 52, Autumn, 1998.

Notes on forthcoming publications and future events, *Richard Wilbur Society Newsletter*, no. 2, Spring, 1999.

For the Love of Books: 115 Celebrated Writers on the Books They Love Most, compiled by Ronald B. Schwartz, Grosset/Putnam, New York, 1999.

Works Edited

Modern American and Modern British Poetry, revised, shorter edition, edited by Louis Untermeyer, in consultation with Karl Shapiro and RW, Harcourt, Brace and Co., New York, 1955.

A Bestiary, illustrated by Alexander Calder, Pantheon, New York, 1955/Fourth Estate, London, 1993.

Edgar Allan Poe, *Poe*, Laurel Poetry Series, Dell, New York, 1959. (RW was also general editor of the series.)

William Shakespeare, *Poems* (The Pelican Shakespeare, AB 37), eds. RW and Alfred Harbage, Penguin Books, Baltimore, Maryland, 1966.

Witter Bynner, *Selected Poems* (a volume in the *Works of Witter Bynner*), Farrar Straus Giroux, New York, 1978.

Works for Children and Light Verse

MOST OF THESE WORKS, THOUGH MARKETED AS CHILDREN'S BOOKS AND CERTAINLY APPEALING TO CHILDREN, ARE NOT LIMITED IN THEIR AUDIENCE. SOME LIGHT VERSE IN THE 'OPPOSITES' FORM WAS CLEARLY WRITTEN FOR AN ADULT AUDIENCE (E.G., ABOUT INDIVIDUALS ON CELEBRATORY OCCASIONS).

Major Book Publications

Loudmouse, Crowell Collier, New York/Collier-Macmillan, London, 1963.
Digging for China, Doubleday and Co., Garden City, New York, 1970.
Opposites, Harcourt Brace Jovanovich, New York, 1973.
More Opposites, Harcourt Brace Jovanovich, New York, 1991.
A Game of Catch, Harcourt Brace Jovanovich, San Diego, California, 1994.
Runaway Opposites, Harcourt, Brace and Co., San Diego, California, 1995.
The Disappearing Alphabet, Harcourt, Brace and Co., San Diego, California, 1998.
Opposites, More Opposites, and Some Differences, Harcourt, San Diego, New York, London, 2000.
The Pig in the Spigot, Harcourt, San Diego, New York, forthcoming, Fall, 2000.

Limited Edition, Private Press, Personal, Broadside, and Similar Publications

Prince Souvanna Phouma: An Exchange between Richard Wilbur & William Jay Smith, Hippogryph Press, Williamstown, Massachusetts, 1963, 100 copies.

Festschrift: A Tribute to Sam Green since 1948, broadside, containing tributes by several people, including six short untitled poems by RW, signed either 'Earl E. Settler' or 'Pie O'Near', 100 copies.

Verses on the Times, light verse colloquy by RW and William Jay Smith, printed for Smith's 60th birthday, 22 April, 1978, 300 copies.

Pedestrian Flight, Palaemon Press, Winston-Salem, North Carolina, 1981, several variants, totalling fewer than 300 copies, one having the imprint 'Privately printed' and used as a Christmas card by the publisher.

From Richard Wilbur, broadside, seven clerihews written for *Eudora Welty: A Tribute,* 1984, 5 copies.

More Opposites, broadside, printed on the occasion of a talk by Jack Hagstrom at the Rowfant Club, Cleveland, January 20, 1988, Sea Cliff Press, New York, 1988, 180 copies, 80 of which were for members of the Club, and 100 for distribution by the Press.

Some Atrocities, Bits Press, Cleveland, Ohio, 1990, 300 copies.

Some Opposites, Nadja, New York, 1990, 100 numbered copies in wrappers, 26 lettered copies, bound.

A Difference, broadside, Parchment Gallery Graphics, Dept. of Humanities, University of Charleston, Charleston, West Virginia, 1996, 99 trade copies, 26 copies *hors commerce,* 10 author's copies. Originally entitled 'Room and Moor', reproduced from RW's fair copy, including a drawing by him.

The Disappearing Alphabet, Catawba Press, Northampton, Massachusetts, 1998.

Uncollected

Six cartoons illustrating André du Bouchet's article, 'Naming the animals', *Child Life,* v. 26, no. 1, January, 1947.

'The Adventure of Hungry Roger', *Child Life,* v. 26, no. 4, April, 1947.

'Animals You *Won't* See at the Circus', five cartoons, *Child Life,* v. 26, no. 5, May, 1947.

Promotional flyer for a production of George Garrett's *Sir Slob,* Alley Theatre, Houston, Texas, March, 1961.

'For George P. Garrett', on a broadside entitled *Happy Birthday, George,* Charlotte, North Carolina, 1979.

'Some Jingles in Honor of Frank Davis', *The Amherst News,* v. 1, no. 4, September 11, 1980, Amherst, Massachusetts.

'What is the Opposite of *Tate*?', first line, 'Celebrating Allen Tate: the Seventy-Fifth Birthday of a Fugitive Poet', by Allen Wigginton Bell, *Vanderbilt Alumnus,* v. 60, no. 3, Spring, 1975.

'Lines Written for Franny Wells on the Occasion of a Testimonial Feast Honoring Him on July 9, 1976', *Stone Walls,* v. 1, no. 3, 1976.

'In the Silver Period Style, Involved and Listless', a single line contributed by RW to 'The Great American Poem', compiled by Philip Dacey, *Antaeus,* no. 32, Winter, 1979.

'Some Differences', 5 poems, 'Dawn and Daybreak'; 'Owl and Cat'; 'Room and Moor'; 'Lips'; 'Footballs and Shoes', *The Massachusetts Review,* v. 22, no. 4, Winter, 1981 (in fact, May, 1982). Reprinted in: *Light Year '84,* ed. Robert Wallace, Bits Press, Cleveland, Ohio, 1983.

'Haiku', *Light Year '84,* ed. Robert Wallace, Bits Press, Cleveland, Ohio, 1983.

'A Jingle for R. McG', *The Little Brown Mouse: A Garland for Robert McGlynn,* ed. John

Failon and John O'Brien, Deerfield Publications, Deerfield, Massachusetts, 1984.
'The Rule', *A Celebration for Stanley Kunitz on His 80th Birthday*, Riverdale-on-Hudson, Sheep Meadow Press, New York, 1986.
'Some Clerihews for John', *John Ciardi: Measure of the Man*, ed. Vince Clemente, University of Arkansas Press, Fayetteville, Arkansas, 1987.
'Double Dactyl, Clerihew, and Ablauted Clerihews', *A Garland for John Hollander*, ed. Natalie Charkow and J. D. McClatchy, Bembo Typographic Co., New York, 1989.
'The Opposite of '42', first line, *Amherst College 1942*, Class of 1942 Reunion book, Amherst, Massachusetts, 1992.
'Two Clerihews for You about Today's Me', written as if by David Slavitt, but actually by RW, David Slavitt, *Slavitt! The Unauthorized Biography*, Exhibitionist Press, Montpelier, Vermont, 1994.
'The Birth of a Verse Form: on the Academic Retirement of Lewis Turco', an exchange of poems with Turco, *Formalist*, v. 8, no. 1, 1997.

INTERVIEWS

MAJOR BOOK PUBLICATIONS

Conversations with Richard Wilbur, ed. William Butts, University of Mississippi Press, Jackson, Mississippi, and London, 1990.

UNCOLLECTED

'Pulitzer Prize-winner Richard Wilbur Wrote Poetry in Foxholes', by Nicholas Zook, *The Worcester Sunday Telegram*, Worcester, Massachusetts, June 16, 1957.
'Poet Abhors Chores and Chooses Muses', by Andrew P. Kopkind, *The Washington Post*, May 5, 1959.
Interview, *Our Times*, v.1, no. 13, January 4, 1961.
'Poets and their Work: Wilbur Describes his Methods', by William K. Wyant, Jr., *St. Louis Post Dispatch*, April 16, 1961.
'Soviet Authors Acquire a New Freedom', *The Register Magazine*, New Haven, Connecticut, November 19, 1961.
Interview, *Talks with Authors*, ed. C. F. Madden, Southern Illinois University Press, Carbondale and Edwardsville, Illinois/Feffer & Simons, London, ©1968.
Interview by Thelma Whiting, *Daily Hampshire Gazette*, Northampton, Massachusetts, August 9, 1968.
'Poetic Order in Chaotic World Goal of Wilbur, Keese Lecturer', by Ewing Carruthers, *The Chattanooga Times*, March 19, 1969.
'Richard Wilbur on Modern Poetry', by Ronald George, *Accent, The Hartford Times Sunday Magazine*, July 20, 1969.
'Separating Bob Dylan from Richard Wilbur', by Neil Davis, *The Hartford Courant Magazine*, May 23, 1971.
'Wesleyan's Poet Wilbur a Molière Fan', by Edward King, *The New Haven Register*, November 7, 1971.
Interview, *Craft So Hard to Learn*, Morrow, New York, 1972.
'The Image and the Object: an Interview with Richard Wilbur', by David Dillon, *Southwest Review*, v. 58, no. 3, Summer, 1973. Reprinted in *American Poetry Observed*, ed. Joe

David Bellamy, University of Illinois Press, Urbana, Illinois,1984.

'Daily Closeup', by Robert Garrett, *New York Post*, February 4, 1975.

'Richard Wilbur: a Poet Speaks', by Diana Loercher, *The Christian Science Monitor*, v. 67, no. 94, April 9, 1975.

'Poet-Translator to Give Reading', by Dennis Brown, *The Plain Dealer*, Cleveland, Ohio, May 22, 1975.

'Adapting for Television', by Deborah P. Butler, *Prime Time 57*, v. 4, no. 5 , May, 1978.

'The Mystery of Things That Are: an Interview with Richard Wilbur', *The Poetry Miscellany*, no. 9, December, 1979.

Interview by Sung Kon Kim, *Literature and Thought*, v. 4, no. 89, April, 1980, pp. 53-64. In Korean.

'Director Wanted Racine Translation – and Poet Had It', by J. Wynn Rousuck, *The Baltimore Sun*, November 29, 1981.

'From French to English: a Conversation with Richard Wilbur', *Performing Arts*, v. 16, no. 5, May, 1982.

Interview excerpts, Peter Brazeau, *Parts of a World: Wallace Stevens Remembered*, Random House, New York, ©1983.

'Captured by Poetry', by Vicki Sanders, *The Miami Herald*, March 11, 1984.

'Letters from Richard Wilbur', *The Hoboken Terminal*, v. 3, no. 2, 1985.

'Richard Wilbur in Conversation with J. D. McClatchy', *PN Review*, v. 13, no. 5, issue 55, March, 1987.

'Richard Wilbur: the Laureate Comes to Light. The Poet on his Craft and His New Position', by Elizabeth Kastor, *The Washington Post*, October 6, 1987.

'Poet Laureateship Allows Wilbur Best of all Worlds', by Ann Geracimos, *The Washington Times*, October 8, 1987.

'Avoiding the Pitfalls of Verse for Hire', by Irvine Molotsky, *The New York Times*, October 27, 1987.

'An Interrupted Interview', by Henry Taylor, edited version of a television interview conducted on May 3, 1988, transcribed by William Butts, *Delos*, v. 3, no. 2, Fall, 1990.

'The Milkweed Speaks', by June Steinberg, *Seattle Weekly*, v. 13, no. 21, May 25, 1988.

'A Lyrical Love Affair with Life', interview by Andrea E. Kehoe, *Washington College Magazine*, v. 36, no. 4, Summer, 1988.

'The Secrets of our Success', by Bill Strickland, *Writer's Digest*, December, 1988, pp. 24-43. Includes two responses by RW.

'Wilbur '42 Adds Second Pulitzer to His Honors', by Jennifer Mathews, *The Amherst Student*, v. 118, no. 23, April 26, 1989.

'Wilbur: a Poet of This World', by Carol Flake, *The Boston Globe*, May 9, 1989.

'America's Prized Poet', by Randall Howe, *Berkshire Week*, June 4-10, 1989.

'Musings of a Poet Laureate', by Jeff O'Heir, *Transcript-Telegram*, Holyoke, Massachusetts, November 25, 1989.

'Wilbur Discusses Poetry During Residence at Amherst', by Lisa Smith, *The Amherst Student*, v. 119, no. 10, November 29, 1989.

Contemporary Authors, new revision series, 29, Gale, Detroit, Michigan, 1990. Includes an interview by Jean Ross within the entry on RW.

Peter Davison, *The Fading Smile: Poets in Boston from Robert Frost to Robert Lowell to Sylvia Plath, 1955-1960*, Knopf, New York, 1994. Includes an interview with RW from July 1, 1991.

'A Moveable Feast', interview by Alex Chadwick and reading on National Public Radio, November 21, 1991. Audio cassette available from NPR.

Interview by Dennis Brown in 'Wordsmiths', chapter 8 of Brown's *Shoptalk*, Newmarket Press, New York, 1992.

'An Interview with Richard Wilbur', by William Baer, *The Formalist*, v. 4, no. 1, 1993.

'A Conversation with Richard Wilbur', by Jewel Spears Brooker, *Christianity and Literature*, v. 42, no. 4, Summer, 1993.

'Babel Questionnaire – Richard Wilbur', *Babel*, no. 8, 1994.

Untitled, portions of RW's interview have been interspersed with portions of others' to form a continuous narrative, Gary Fountain and Peter Brazeau, *Remembering Elizabeth Bishop: An Oral Biography*, University of Massachusetts Press, Amherst, Massachusetts, 1994.

'An Interview with Richard Wilbur', by Rick Carson, *Georgia State University Review*, Spring, 1994.

'Richard Wilbur on W. H. Auden', *The W. H. Auden Society Newsletter*, no. 12, April, 1994.

'From Amherst College to U.S. Poet Laureate', by Dan Salzstein, *The Amherst Student*, May 22, 1994.

'A Conversation with Richard Wilbur', by Paul Mariani, *Image*, no. 12, Winter, 1995-96.

'Translating Past into Present', by Michael Blowen, *The Boston Globe*, August 4, 1996.

'Interview with Richard Wilbur', in *Speaking of Frost: Richard Wilbur and William H. Pritchard interviewed by Donald G. Sheehy*, Friends of the Amherst College Library, Amherst, Massachusetts, 1997. Excerpts appear on the CD, *Robert Frost: Poems, Life, Legacy*, noted below under video recordings.

'Richard Wilbur: an Interview', by Joseph T. Cox, *War, Literature & the Arts*, v. 10, no. 1, Spring/Summer, 1998.

'Norman Mailer and Richard Wilbur', by Robert Lucid, *The Paris Review*, no. 150, Spring, 1999.

RECORDINGS

LISTED HERE ARE COMMERCIALLY AVAILABLE RECORDINGS OF BOTH RW SPEAKING OR READING HIS OWN OR OTHERS' POEMS, AND READINGS OF RW'S POEMS BY OTHERS. WE HAVE NOT INCLUDED THOSE THAT, ALTHOUGH NOT PUBLISHED IN THE USUAL SENSE, ARE AVAILABLE FOR PURCHASE, E.G. FROM THE LIBRARY OF CONGRESS (WHERE THE CURRENT CATALOGUE LISTS APPROXIMATELY 100 RW RECORDINGS; ONLY A VERY FEW WERE PUBLISHED IN THE CONVENTIONAL SENSE). WE HAVE INDICATED THE FORMAT OR FORMATS KNOWN TO US TO EXIST FOR EACH RECORDING, BUT IT IS ENTIRELY POSSIBLE THAT A REISSUE IN LATER FORMAT EXISTS EVEN IF NOT NOTED (E.G., A CD REISSUE OF A CASSETTE ORIGINAL). WE HAVE ALSO NOT INCLUDED RECORDINGS OF MUSICAL SETTINGS OF RW'S POEMS, OR OF *CANDIDE*, TO WHICH HE CONTRIBUTED MANY LYRICS, OR OF DRAMATIC PRODUCTIONS OF RW'S TRANSLATIONS OF MOLIÈRE AND RACINE.

AUDIO

New England Anthology, no. 6, RW and John Ciardi, Literary Society of the University of Massachusetts, Amherst, Massachusetts, 1954, LP, cassette.

Gene Derwood, *The Poems of Gene Derwood: An Anthology of Poets' Voices*, reading by RW and others, Spoken Arts, New York, 1955, LP, 736.

Caedmon Treasury of Modern Poets Reading Their Own Poetry, Caedmon, ©1957, 2 cassettes, CDL52006.

Richard Wilbur Reads His Poems, Pacifica Tape Library, Berkeley, California, 1957, cassette, AD0291.

Many Voices: Adventures in Appreciation, narrated by RW, to accompany a textbook, Harcourt, Brace, New York, 1958, 2 LPs.

The Poems of Richard Wilbur, read by RW, Spoken Arts, New Rochelle, New York, 1959,

LP, 747, cassette, 747. Reissued as no. 5 in v. 1 of *Twentieth Century Poets*, cassette, 7138-M. Apparently also in *20th Century Poets Read Their Work*, 6 cassettes, PCC20.

Anthology of Contemporary American Poetry, includes two poems by RW, read by George Abbe, Folkways, New York, 1961, LP, FL9735.

Twentieth Century Poetry in English: Nine Pulitzer Prize Poets Reading Their Own Poems, Library of Congress, Washington, D.C., 1963, LP, PL29.

Andrei Voznesensky, *Antiworlds*, read in Russian by the poet and in English by his translators, including RW, Columbia, New York, 1966, LP, OL6590.

Poets for Peace, Spoken Arts, New Rochelle, New York, 1968, LP, SA990.

Richard Wilbur Reading His Poetry, Caedmon, New York, 1968, LP, TC1248, cassette, CDL51248.

Carol Channing Reads and Sings, includes RW's *Loudmouse*, Caedmon, New York, ©1969, LP, TC1305, cassette, CDL51305.

A Game of Catch, Ginn & Co., New York, ©1969, record 5 of a set, *Voices 2*, to accompany a textbook, LP.

America's Poets: Richard Wilbur, reading by RW and discussion with Barry Ulanov, Center for Cassette Studies, Hollywood, California, 1971, 2 cassettes, 10172-73.

Robert Lowell & Richard Wilbur: Two Pulitzer Prize Winners Read from and Discuss Their Works, Center for Cassette Studies, Hollywood, California, 1971, cassette.

Yevgeni Yevtushenko, *Yevtushenko in Readings from His New York and San Francisco Poetry Concerts*, includes reading by RW of his translations, Columbia, New York, 1972, LP, S31344.

Contemporary Poets Reading Their Own Works, v. 2, no. 6, Caedmon, New York, 1972, cassette, CDL51248.

Cricket and Other Friends, includes RW reading some of his short poems in the form he invented known as 'opposites', Open Court, La Salle, Illinois, ©1974, LP.

The Spoken Arts Treasury of 100 Modern American Poets Reading Their Poems, v. 14, Meredith, Swenson, Nemerov, Ferlinghetti, RW, Moss, Spoken Arts, New Rochelle, New York, ©1985, LP, SA1053, cassette, SAC1053.

Richard Wilbur, reading at the Pierpont Morgan Library, introduced by James Merrill, Academy of American Poets, New York, 1989, cassette.

Amherst College Glee Clubs, 1935-1977, compiled by Amherst College Hurricane Class of 1942, 55th Reunion, includes remarks and reading by RW, from an earlier, unidentified source.

VIDEO

A Game of Catch, Witty-Siris Productions, distributed by Macmillan Films, 1973, 16 mm film.

Robert Frost, Voices & Visions, Intellimation, Santa Barbara, California, 1987, 16 mm film, VHS, Beta, or U-matic cassette.

A Conversation with Richard Wilbur, an interview by Grace Cavalieri, Library of Congress, Washington, D.C., 1989, VHS cassette.

Richard Wilbur, reading, with an interview by David St. John, Lannan Foundation, Los Angeles, California, 1990, Lannan Literary Videos, 16, VHS cassette.

A Game of Catch, Pyramid Film & Video, Santa Monica, California, 1990, VHS cassette.

Off the Page: The First Video Poetry Magazine, v. 1, no. 1, includes reading by RW, Prima Donna Productions, Fairfield, New Jersey, 1991, VHS cassette.

Herman Melville: Consider the Sea, hosted by RW, International Film Bureau, Chicago, Illinois, 1982, 16 mm film, videocassette, 1/2 in. or 3/4 in. Reissued: Monterey Home Video, Malibu, California, 1995, VHS cassette, 31517.

Robert Frost: Poems, Life, Legacy, narrated by RW, who is also interviewed, Holt, New York, 1997, CD-ROM.

SECONDARY WORKS

THE SECONDARY LITERATURE ON RW'S WORK IS FAR TOO EXTENSIVE TO BE LISTED HERE. IT HAS BEEN THOROUGHLY COVERED BY FRANCES BIXLER'S WORK, DETAILS OF WHICH ARE GIVEN IN THE BIBLIOGRAPHIES SECTION BELOW. HERE WE LIST ONLY BOOK-LENGTH TREATMENTS OF RW'S WORK.

Donald L. Hill, *Richard Wilbur,* Twayne's United States Authors Series, 117, Twayne, New York, 1967.
Paul Cummins. *Richard Wilbur: A Critical Essay,* Contemporary Writers in Christian Perspective series, Eerdmans, Grand Rapids, Michigan, 1971.
Richard Wilbur's Creation, ed. Wendy Salinger, Under Discussion Series, University of Michigan Press, Ann Arbor, Michigan, 1983.
Bruce Michelson, *Wilbur's Poetry: Music in a Scattering Time,* University of Massachusetts Press, Amherst, Massachusetts, 1991.
Rodney Stenning Edgecombe, *A Reader's Guide to the Poetry of Richard Wilbur,* University of Alabama Press, Tuscaloosa, Alabama, and London, 1995.
John B. Hougen, *Ecstasy Within Discipline: The Poetry of Richard Wilbur,* American Academy of Religion, Academy Series, 85, Scholars Press, Atlanta, Georgia, 1995.

BIBLIOGRAPHIES

John Field, *Richard Wilbur: a Bibliographical Checklist,* The Serif Series, Bibliographies and Checklists, 16, Kent State University Press, Kent, Ohio, 1971.
Bixler, Frances, *Richard Wilbur: a Reference Guide,* G. K. Hall, Boston, Massachusetts, 1991. Supplemented by Frances Bixler and Jane Hoogestraat, 'Richard Purdy Wilbur: a Review of the Research and Criticism', *Resources for American Literary Study,* v. 20, no. 1, 1994, and Bruce Michelson, 'Recent publications about Richard Wilbur (1993-Present)', in *The Richard Wilbur Society Newsletter,* no. 2, Spring, 1999.

THE WILBUR ARCHIVES

Most of RW's papers are located at the Robert Frost Library, Amherst College, Massachusetts. These include manuscripts relating to *Ceremony, Things of this World, Advice to a Prophet,* and *Walking to Sleep.*

Additional manuscripts, relating to early work, are located in the Poetry Collection, Lockwood Memorial Library, State University of New York at Buffalo.

The Critics

'Your own things have a fine freedom about them notwithstanding your interest in form: I mean freedom from tripe and trash. The fact that you delight in exercising that freedom means more than anything else.'

– Wallace Stevens, letter to RW, July 26, 1946

'Wilbur's immaculate verbal choice, his freshening of the sense of life within a rigid metrical frame and not only within it but by means of it, recall Frost's writing at its best.'

– Robert Fitzgerald, review of *The Beautiful Changes*, New Republic, 1949

'Mr Wilbur never goes too far, but he never goes far enough. In the most serious sense of the word he is not a very satisfactory poet. And yet he seems the best of the quite young poets writing in this century, poets considerably younger than Lowell and Bishop and Shapiro and Roethke and Schwartz.'

– Randall Jarrell, review of *Ceremony*, 1950

'If when the Guggenheim Awards are announced Richard Wilbur is not named, I should like to suggest him for your consideration.'

– Wallace Stevens, letter to Norman Holmes Pearson, January 24, 1952

'Richard Wilbur is the wisest, wittiest, cleverest, finest of poets establishing their careers in this country.'

– Paul Engle, review of *Things of this World*, Chicago Sunday Tribune, 1956

'The world of the younger poets, at present, certainly is the world of Richard Wilbur and safer paler mirror-images of Richard Wilbur – who'd have thought that the era of the poet in the Grey Flannel Suit was coming?'

– Randall Jarrell, letter to Elizabeth Bishop, 1956

'Richard Wilbur I know only by four poems in *The Penguin Book of Modern American Verse*, one of which, "Death of a Toad", I like very much indeed.'

– Philip Larkin, letter to Donald Hall, 1956

'Mr Wilbur, one of the most famous of the younger American poets, is a deliberately rich, variegated, and ornate writer ... a superb verse craftsman who makes most of his English contemporaries – those between 30-40 – look like fumbling amateurs ...'

– G. S. Fraser, review of *Poems, 1943-1956, New Statesman,* 1957

'The civil grace and conscience of art, handsomely controlled, can by this time be taken for granted in the work of Richard Wilbur. From the very first he has shown himself to be a master of form ...'

– Dudley Fitts, review of *Advice to a Prophet and Other Poems,*
New York Times Book Review, 1961

'[One has] the feeling that the cleverness of phrase and the delicious aptness of Wilbur's poems sometimes mask an unwillingness or inability to think or feel deeply, that the poems tend to lapse toward highly sophisticated play ...

If someone is already the most charming and amiable man in the world, there's no need for him to try to be something or somebody else.'

– James Dickey, review of *Advice to a Prophet, Sewanee Review,* 1962,

'In contrast [to Berryman] was Richard Wilbur's *The Beautiful Changes,* which was the peak of skilful elegance ... Many poets after Wilbur resembled him, and some of them were good at it, but the typical ghastly poem of the fifties was a Wilbur poem not written by Wilbur ... (It wasn't Wilbur's fault, though I expect he will be asked to suffer for it.)'

– Donald Hall, Introduction to *Contemporary American Poetry,* 1962

'Petronius spoke of the "studied felicity" of Horace's poetry, and I can never read one of Richard Wilbur's books without thinking of this phrase. His impersonal, exactly accomplished, faintly sententious skill produces poems that, ordinarily, compose themselves into a little too regular a beauty ... and yet "A Baroque Wall-Fountain in the Villa Sciarra" is one of the most marvellously beautiful, one of the most nearly perfect poems any American has written, and poems like "A Black November Turkey" and "A Hole in the Floor" are the little differentiated, complete-in-themselves universes that true works of art are. Wilbur's lyric calling-to-life of the things of this world – the things, rather than the processes or the people – specializes in both true and false happy endings, not by choice but by necessity; he obsessively sees, and shows, the bright underside of every dark thing.'

– Randall Jarrell, 'Fifty Years of American Poetry', 1962

'*Advice to a Prophet* is a constant pleasure. Every poem here has a clear structure of orderly description, illustrated thought, or controlled fancy ... the sensuousness, the sense and the weight of each of these poems is perfectly judged...'

– Anonymous review of *Advice to a Prophet, The Times,* 1962

' ... there is no personal source anywhere, as there is no passion and no insanity; the insistent

"I", the asserting of sex, and the flaunting of madness considered apparently in equally bad taste.'

— Leslie Fiedler, *Waiting for the End*, 1964

'The translator of Molière must be elegant, witty, supple: able to write formal and polished couplets that retain speech rhythms. No living poet is better able to do this than Mr Wilbur, who has the technical mastery and – at times – the bite of Pope himself.'

— Laurence Lerner, *The Listener*, 1964

'I have just shelved ['On Poetry and Happiness'] with Criticism, in a case behind this chair. ... You come between Valéry & Edmund Wilson, and you dignify the company. I wish you wrote prose more often, my friend, you make most critics, including me, look like drudges.'

— John Berryman, Letter to RW, 1970

'In the vast number of his successful poems, we encounter a civilized man struggling to strike a "difficult balance" between freedom and form, spontaneity and tradition, between the religious aspiration contained in St Peter's Fountain and the secular ecstasy contained in "The Baroque Wall Fountain, Villa Sciarra". He will often give us a lovely picture of a beautifully symmetrical garden, but he will never let us forget that "the garden of the world ... escape[s] our simpler symmetries".'

— Paul F. Cummins, *Richard Wilbur: a Critical Essay*, 1971

'Wilbur can no more change direction than a tree can. He is a nature poet, in the sense that he uses natural growths and objects: trees, ferns, stones (but interestingly enough seldom animals) as his subject matter... I know of no one writing today who uses English with such balance, purpose and delight.'

— Shirley Toulson, review of *Walking to Sleep, Poetry Review*,1971

'As Wilbur solidified his position, the general run of his poetry slipped past limpidity and got closer to torpor. By the time of *Advice to a Prophet* self-parody was creeping in ...
Yet with all this taken into account, there is still no reason to think that Wilbur will not eventually come up with something. At present he is off balance, a condition he is constitutionally unfitted to exploit. While he was on balance, though, he wrote a good number of poised, civilized and very beautiful poems. They'll be worth remembering when some of the rough, tough, gloves-off stuff we're lately supposed to admire starts to look thin. The beautiful changes ... but I don't think it changes into *Crow*.'

— Clive James, review of *Walking to Sleep, The Review*,1971

'Wilbur: can look at a thing, and talk about it beautifully, can turn it over in his mind, and draw truths from a scene, easily and effortlessly (it would seem) – though this kind of writing requires the hardest kind of discipline, it must be remembered. Not a graceful mind – that's a mistake – but a mind of grace, an altogether different and higher thing.'

— Theodore Roethke, notebook entry, 1972

'[Wilbur's] degree of accuracy [as a translator] is almost always very high and his technical skill as a poet is just about equal to that of the people he translates.'

— Raymond Oliver, 'Verse Translation and Richard Wilbur', *Southern Review*, 1975

'This morning when your *Mind Reader* came in the mail, I felt I was visiting another country, not too distant from mine [in *Day by Day*] and with similar flashes – night and waking thoughts; age ... nature and household description. What struck me as different and enviable is your pace ... You fix on it slowly and hesitantly – poking and puzzling. Your strict metres speak casually. All this is a good antidote to my narrower intensity. I think we both try for a fairly direct open language – open to experience, and open at times to splurges of rhetoric and intuition. Your style is perhaps a commentary or extension of Frost; or rather your draw on something earlier that he could use but is now almost unavailable to anyone but you – among other things an oblique use of autobiography, scenes peering into meditation.'

— Robert Lowell, letter to RW, 1976

'Let me try to list some of the virtues that distinguish the poetry of Richard Wilbur. First of all, a superb ear (unequalled, I think, in the work of any poet now writing in English) for stately measure, cadences of a slow, processional grandeur, and rich, ceremonial orchestration. His "musicianship" is of so fine and conspicuous a kind that it has often been ignored, and sometimes mocked by those who are militantly tone-deaf. Next, a philosophic bent and a religious temper, which are by no means the same thing, but which here consort comfortably together. Wit, polish, a formal elegance that is never haughty or condescending, though, again, by those unimpressed by or envious of his skills it is taken for a chilling frigidity. And an unfeigned gusto, a naturally happy and grateful response to the physical beauty of the world, of women, of works of art, landscapes, weather, and his perceiving, constructing mind that tries to know them. But in a way I think most characteristic of all, his is the most kinetic poetry I know: verbs are among his decisively important tools, and his poetry is everywhere a vision of action, of motion and performance.

... in this poetic era of arrogant solipsism and limp narcissism – when great shaggy herds of poets write only about themselves, or about the casual workings of their rather tedious minds – it is essential to our sanity, salutary to our humility, and a minimal obeisance to the truth to acknowledge, with Wilbur, in poem after poem ... the vast alterity, the "otherness" of the world, that huge corrective to our self-sufficiency.'

— Anthony Hecht, review of *The Mind Reader*, *TLS*, 1977

'Wilbur's chief recurrent theme is implicit in his approach to style. His intricately patterned poems reflect the discovery of patterns of natural beauty; and the poet's art thus strives to be an adequate analogy to the surrounding creation. The art of man mirrors the art of God. Creative energy finding its expression in natural and aesthetic form is what Wilbur continually contemplates, praises, and seeks to realize in his own writing. Such a concern, and

Wilbur's treatment of it, may broadly be described as Catholic. I say this without reference to Wilbur's religious affiliation, of which I have no knowledge. Perhaps a better word is "sacramental": the poems at their deepest level are acts of sacramental perception, with similarities in thought (though few in style) to the lyrics of Hopkins, which also treat of the created universe as an outward sign and token of an inward and spiritual grace. Certainly Wilbur is more reticent of dogmatizing than Hopkins; confession of faith is not his prime motive in writing. But the Jesuit's homemade term for the patterned signatures of grace in nature, *inscape*, is one which happily defines the object of Wilbur's imagination. Through an intensity of focus he suggests the informing spiritual energy present in the appearances that capture his attention.'

– Robert B. Shaw, review of *The Mind Reader, Parnassus,* 1977

'In Wilbur's finished poems there are no overwhelming passions, none of the gestures at raw experience which characterize the work of some of his contemporaries, nor does he support his poems with elaborate explications and apologetics which mask a deficient technique. His poems balance contradictory impulses and emotions, they are contexts in which emotion is not merely expressed but related and realized.'

– Peter Jones, *An Introduction to 50 American Poets,* 1979

'For Richard Wilbur, the sights offered by World War II contradict and threaten his most basic beliefs, as we can infer them from his writings: that love is more powerful than hatred; that nature is a source of values and of reassurance; and that there is a strong creative urge in both man and nature which constantly seeks and finds expression in images of graceful plenitude.'

– John Reibetanz, *Modern Poetry Studies,* 1982

'What Wilbur stands for in my mind is a certain grave elegance of spirit, inseparable from the formal beauty of his verse ... Wilbur's mind has a cleansing unity and wit that makes it possible for him to view the world, despite its manifest burden of suffering and injustice and evil, as a place of fortuitous joys and blessings and miracles, not the least of which is the gift of life itself. He has conducted himself, in his work as in his days, with humour and decency and dignity. His poems tell of his love for the things of this world, and his clear-eyed scrutiny of particulars puts us on the path that leads to universals.'

– Stanley Kunitz, introducing a reading by RW at the Guggenheim Museum, New York, December 14, 1983

'This, then, was Wilbur's first style, which dazzled and fetched so many readers. If he did not subsequently change his way of writing as remarkably as Rich, Merrill, and other contemporaries, he nevertheless developed a plainer style and, in some poems a greater emotional intensity.'

–David Perkins, *History of Modern Poetry,* 1987

'If Robert Frost has an authentic living heir, it is probably Wilbur – particularly as the poet of the short lyric in strict and familiar metres who speaks in the middle voice, wittily and movingly, to a wide audience.'

– Joseph H. Summers, *Reference Guide to American Literature*, 1987

'Among the honourable schoolboys of American poetry, Richard Wilbur has often seemed the most cursed by his talent. Clever as a cat, aseptically witty, gifted in the methods of his masters, he was able in his earliest work to charm his way into favour or chatter out of difficulty. Though most poets eventually leave their sugared sonnets and their scandals behind, a few ... remain schoolboys into old age, a sly immaturity coexisting happily with the more mature forms of ague and argument.

To suggest that Wilbur is of that company recognizes his peculiar attractions as well as his particular limitations. *New and Collected Poems* ... does nothing to alter the shape of a career as honoured as it has been honourable. The poet laureateship to which he was appointed last year is a bit of American Anglophilia, barely more serious than naming a state insect or a state reptile. Though earned for books published over thirty years ago, the honour was not misplaced.

Wilbur's most brilliant and ambitious work ... was done young. What earlier seemed playful gradually hardened, and the coolly detached tone became complacent and plummy, especially in the shorter poems scattered throughout his books ... As the intensity of Wilbur's poetry subsided, his attention turned to translation, to which we owe the incomparable renditions of Molière and Racine.

With Anthony Hecht and James Merrill, Wilbur maintained a formal tradition when even the word "tradition" was suspect. Of the poets of his generation, those born in the decade after World War I, he is among the two or three most vital and surely the most elegant. Randall Jarrell once wrote in a letter, "Not that I don't like Wilbur, but one is enough". No reader will be ungrateful for that one.'

– William Logan, review of *New and Collected Poems, Chicago Tribune*, 1988

'Even Richard Wilbur, one of our finest living poets, is drawn to indirection, exotic words and cultural poems. Hence his poems on crickets is not entitled 'Crickets' or 'Cicadas' but 'Cigales'. And he cannot resist writing 'A Baroque Wall-Fountain in the Villa Sciarra', a poem whose title tells a story. These poems are hardly without their virtues. But it is worth noting that they are the virtues of a gentile cultural elite, their breeding ground the English Departments of the '50s with their Fulbright overseas scholarships and their valorization of wit, irony and complexity, the legacy of the New Critics.'

– Robert McPhillips, *Crosscurrents*, 1988

'The poetry of Richard Wilbur ... has long been recognized as being graceful and technically accomplished. The publication of his *New and Collected Poems* is therefore an occasion to celebrate ... If it were not for writers like him, future students might wonder if there were no poets in the late 20th century who championed beauty ... or who were capable of rising above all the despair and doubt. Fortunately, we do have Richard Wilbur, and I am confident our age will be deemed better for it.'

– Robert Richman, review of *New and Collected Poems,*
New York Times Book Review, 1988

'I then found in my reading of Richard Wilbur, and Elizabeth Bishop, the most useful models of the speed, grace, humour, and descriptive clarity that I tried and am still trying to achieve.'

– Robert B. Shaw, *Crosscurrents*, 1988

'Through difficult and fragmented times, Richard Wilbur, Philip Larkin, and Thom Gunn have written, each in his own way, with beauty and integrity. Their poems are widely known and rightly treasured, and will loom larger and larger in our language as time passes.'

– Timothy Steele, *Crosscurrents*, 1988

'Wilbur's youthful poems "took off" into abstraction from something sharply seen or heard: the flight seemed irresistible.
　Later on, though, we would begin to see why he was being drawn more and more to translation as a means of energising his technical adroitness and his brilliant way with words. He had begun to scratch around for things to take off from.'

– Ian Hamilton, review of *New and Collected Poems*, *TLS*, 1989

' ... I don't think critics have sufficiently noted Wilbur's extraordinary command of small details, which have a prominent place in his later poems. In a brook, he watches "A startled inchling trout / Of spotted near-transparency, / Trawling a shadow solider than he". The fall twilight "darkens like a fast-reducing broth, / Simmering the shape of things." At a party, "the beaked ladle plies the chuckling ice". Everything has been minutely scrutinized and described with a precision that can startle. And he can make of these details, in gestures stately or homely, many memorable images.
　Wilbur's poems do not especially gain by being read in bulk – as, say, Lowell's do. Each of his best poems is a richness to be savoured, not gobbled with the rest. But [*New and Collected Poems*] is a welcome convenience, and I hope it helps discourage those readers who with faint praise classify Wilbur as merely a representative poet, the spokesman for a period or an aesthetic. There are poems throughout this book that will take any preconception by surprise, poems – we realize with sudden joy – that we've had in mind and by heart for years, the first sign than a book is likely to remain a classic.'

– J. D. McClatchy, 'Chiselled Breath', *Partisan Review*, 1990

'Wilbur leaves the text at a distance with his 'virtuous flames' and 'haughty foes' and can seem a little bland, like Dryden on auto-pilot, but there is a case for his approach. It reads easily, and not everyone will want their Racine metamorphosed to the British Raj.'

– John Saunders, review of RW's *Phèdre*, *Stand*, 1989

'What is the truth about Alceste...? Richard Wilbur, who has accomplished the miracle of making Alceste speak American verse, has a subtly balanced estimate that seems to me a touch too severe ...'

– Harold Bloom, *The Western Canon*, 1994

'*Candide* was virtually completed in August 1956. It was Bernstein's most substantial achievement as a composer. The score consists of close to two hours of music and over thirty numbers: solos, duets, trios, quartets, ensembles, choruses and purely orchestral music, frequently interspersed or combined with spoken dialogue. Thanks to Richard Wilbur, *Candide* is impeccably versified.'

– Humphrey Burton, *Leonard Bernstein*, 1994

'The generation of Wilbur gave metre a bad name largely because it did not do much with metre that had not already been done by Auden, Stevens and Ransom.'

– Alan Williamson, *Essays on the Art of Poetry*, 1994

'A number of features of 1950s verse are epitomized in [Wilbur's] style. His poems are deliberately ornate, obviously rich in consonance and assonance, superficially indebted to Hopkins. His language is insistently figurative. Everything is seen in terms of something else – "this mad *instead*", he calls it in a self-critical moment. To emblems, similes, and pretty phrases, he is devoted – to just those types of figurative language that make no claim to spontaneity or sudden revelation. His poems constantly offer the charm of wit, but rarely the force of conviction.'

– Robert von Hallberg, *The Cambridge History of American Literature*, 1996

'[Wilbur] stands apart from his literary age in at least three ways: he exhibits a classic, objective sensibility in a romantic, subjective time; he is a formalist in the midst of relentless informality; and he is a relative optimist among absolute pessimists.'

– Peter Stitt, *Oxford Companion to 20th-Century Poetry*, 1996

'The only translators who seem to have an impeccable sense for Dante's meanings, metre and rhymes – in short, for the total magic of Dante's musicality – are Wilbur and Barnstone, and they have given us but one single canto each. Sigh!'

– Douglas R. Hofstadter, *Le Ton Beau de Marot*, 1997